If the Churches Want World Peace

THE MACMILLAN COMPANY
NEW YORK · CHICAGO
DALLAS · ATLANTA · SAN FRANCISCO
LONDON · MANILA

IN CANADA
BRETT-MACMILLAN LTD.
GALT, ONTARIO

If
The
Churches
Want World Peace

Norman Hill *Llewellyn*, *1895 –*

and

Doniver A. Lund

New York

THE MACMILLAN COMPANY

1958

First Printing

Printed in the United States of America

Library of Congress catalog card number: 58-11542

Preface

The finest qualities of our national character were nurtured in the Christian faith. To criticize the exponents of that faith—the churches and their leaders—is therefore a task which a conscientious layman will not lightly assume. This volume turns a critical eye on the peace efforts of the churches, not to show up failures, but to make a candid assessment of their endeavors and to submit suggestions for improvement. The churches have a role to play in foreign affairs, but not the one in which they have usually cast themselves. The activities of only the Protestant churches are examined in this book, mainly for the reason that those of the Catholic church are carried on in a very different way.

The reader is entitled to know the background of the authors. Dr. Doniver Lund is an active Lutheran and a professor of history in a Lutheran college, Gustavus Adolphus College. His chief contribution to this volume is the research data provided in the Ph.D. thesis which he wrote at the University of Nebraska in 1955, dealing with the peace programs of the churches prior to World War II.

Although I, Norman Hill (the senior partner), was brought up the son of a Baptist clergyman, I have since become a member of the Presbyterian Church. For well over thirty years I have been a professor of international relations, and during that time I have had many personal contacts with the peace movement within the churches, usually on the local level. Serving as a member of Dr.

v

Lund's examining committee at the University of Nebraska, I saw in his thesis a great deal of useful data on church activities in foreign affairs, a subject on which I had already been working for some time. With his research material and my own, which centered mainly on the period from 1939 down to the present, I wrote this book. When I consulted Dr. Lund, I found that he agreed with the points of view which I had advanced and was glad to have his name associated with them.

The approach followed in this book is that of the social scientist, interested primarily in means and methods available for the improvement of society, in this case the world society of nations. No effort has been made to dabble in the theological issues which might be raised as to the proper place of the churches in foreign affairs.

Much of the information gathered together by Dr. Lund and myself on the work of the churches has been taken from religious periodicals; the *Christian Century*, the *Christian Advocate*, and the *Ecumenical Review* were particularly useful. Other sources include the official minutes of the governing bodies of various denominations, a variety of pamphlet materials, and some unpublished studies of individual denominations.

It is a pleasure to acknowledge the help supplied by the staff of the Library of the University of Nebraska. My indebtedness to my wife for her careful reading of the manuscript and for her constructive comments is also acknowledged with gratitude.

NORMAN HILL

Contents

I

A Determined Church

"What can the churches *do* about it?" is a question with which every speaker on international problems is confronted by audiences of Christian workers. The determination to do something about it explains why the Protestant churches of America are today busily at work in behalf of a durable peace. They feel "the breath of history upon their faces," as Dr. Walter Van Kirk, a leader in the movement, has said. Their deep commitment to the cause was recognized by Secretary-General Dag Hammarskjold in 1954, when he declared, "The churches and the United Nations have an aim in common and a field of action where they work side by side." That it was Section IV on International Affairs at the Evanston Assembly of the World Council of Churches (1954) which served as the "nerve center" of the conference testifies further to the extent of Christian preoccupation with war and peace.

As far back as St. Augustine in the fifth century, Catholic churchmen wrestled with the problem of war, trying to determine the conditions under which, if at all, a Christian may take up arms. To such churchmen as Francisco de Vitoria (1480–1546) and Francisco Suárez (1548–1617) must go credit, too, for promoting the cause of modern international law during the early years of its growth. The mediatory and arbitral activities of the Pope in behalf of peace over a span of several centuries must also be recognized. This Catholic tradition of interest in world affairs was not matched by the Protestant churches, except for a few of the smaller denomi-

1

nations with pacifist tendencies, like the Quakers, until World War I. Individual clergymen had spoken out from time to time on domestic or foreign issues, as did Henry Ward Beecher against slavery and for the Union cause, but the churches themselves remained aloof.

The event that shook all Americans, whether Christian or non-Christian, out of indifference toward world affairs was World War I. Here for the first time was a war of people against people, a war demanding mass hatreds to perpetrate mass murders. It was a war which twisted the economies of nations, uprooted social and political systems, and left behind it impoverished human beings and a world vexed with fascism, communism, and strife. War had always been a nuisance, sometimes a great hardship, but never before had its claims on humanity been so monopolistic. A few men like the German von Clausewitz in the early nineteenth century had foreseen the possibility of total war, but none had experienced it or had even imagined how hideous it could be. Here was a type of war that would subordinate everything to its purposes, including the minds of men and the tenets of the church.

Total war places the Christian church on the defensive. Its outbreak reflects the absence of those Christian virtues which enable peoples to get along with one another—unselfishness, trust, love, and compassion. Its prosecution in battle calls for hatreds and murder. Its aftermath is disillusionment and a heyday for loose living. Becoming increasingly convinced, as World War I wore on, that war is a religious problem, the Protestant churches decided that the time had come for them to play an active part in international relations.

This determination to get rid of war was by no means confined to the churches; inspired by Wilsonian idealism, Americans generally began crusading for an enduring peace. With a nobility of purpose, the churches reached out to take the lead in the movement. As they analyzed it, the cause was one with ethical implications and therefore suited to the kind of leadership which they could provide.

International developments since World War I have emphasized further the moral and spiritual demands of international relations.

World War II demonstrated once again the waste, moral as well as material, of modern war and its inevitable aftermath of discord and disillusionment. The A-bomb dropped by the United States on Hiroshima toward the end of the war reverberated the world over, a portent to all thoughtful men of the disasters ahead if they did not learn to live together harmoniously. The recent invention of still more destructive weapons has made commonplace the remark that the next war will decimate the earth's population, if it does not destroy the planet or make it uninhabitable. Now it is abundantly clear that, as the Amsterdam Assembly of the World Council of Churches said in 1948, war is a "sin against God and a degradation of man," an institution "incompatible with the teaching and example of our Lord Jesus Christ."

Responsible statesmen and historians have frequently recognized the demands which modern international relations place upon the moral and spiritual qualities of mankind. President Truman told a Baptist World Congress in 1950 that "the nations of the world—our own included, with its unprecedented wealth and unlimited resources—cannot survive materially unless redeemed spiritually." Speaking to the World Christian Endeavor Convention in 1954, President Eisenhower asserted that " . . . weapons of war can produce no lasting peace," and "Only a great moral crusade to determine that men shall rise above the conception of materialism, rise above it and live as people who attempt to express in some faint and feeble way their conceptions of what the Almighty would have us do" can give the world a lasting prosperity and peace. Drawing upon his study of earlier civilizations, Professor Arnold Toynbee has pointed to the contributions which religion can make today in the preservation of Western civilization: not a return to orthodoxy but "something novel is demanded," so he has explained, "a venture into the areas of the moral and the spiritual."

More than ever before, then, the moral and spiritual prerequisites of peace are now acknowledged. The pre-World War II approach to the problem of war stressed the mechanical—a League of Nations, a Pact of Paris, or a disarmament conference. While such mechanical arrangements still have the attention of reformers, more and more it is realized that machinery can do little unless supported by peoples. The man on the street, therefore, has become increasingly the objective of the crusader. On Sunday the crusading church has this man in its pews, where he can be reached with moral and religious ideas applicable to the world of nations. The church feels that it would shirk a duty were it to fail to capitalize on this opportunity.

Attention is often directed to the larger reliance of the masses upon the churches in these times of international insecurity and widespread fear, with a hope, apparently, that somewhere in the truths of Christianity will be found light to dispel the darkness. The National Council of Churches of Christ in the United States announced on September 9, 1956, that for the first time in our history more than 100,000,000 persons were affiliated with churches or synagogues. It pointed out that in 1955 there was an increase in church membership of 2.8 per cent as compared with an increase of 1.8 per cent in the nation's population. The National Council's report shows that Sunday and Sabbath school enrollment increased in 1955 by 3.4 per cent to a new high of 38,921,033. Comparative statistics released by the Council show 36 per cent of the population affiliated with churches in 1900, 49 per cent in 1940, 57 per cent in 1950, and 60.9 per cent at the end of 1955. Per capita contributions to the churches are reported as 7 per cent higher in 1955 than in the preceding year. Is it not significant that this revival of religious interest has come at a time when Americans feel helpless in the insecurity of the cold war and in the recurring danger of a hot war? Is it not reasonable to regard this recourse to the churches on the part of a fearful people as a vote of confidence in Christianity's ability to help them through troublesome times?

The nature of the communist threat is another reason why the churches feel the urge to play a role in international affairs. They know full well that a communist-controlled world would have no place for them. Communist dogma, as they are aware, has opposed religion since the time of Karl Marx, regarding it as an opiate which enables the masses to endure the hardships and privations of the capitalist system. When politically expedient, a communist dictator will temporize with religion, as in Soviet Russia, but he will never encourage it. Knowing these facts, and being anxious to retain their own religious freedom as well as that of other peoples, the churches feel the need to concern themselves with current developments in world affairs and in American foreign policy. They look upon themselves as an interested party, with much to gain or to lose from the decisions of policy makers.

Quite possibly, too, the churches harbor something of a guilt complex in international matters, of which they hope to rid themselves by their present absorption with world problems. Certainly it is no credit to them that the war system of today grew up and has worked its greatest havoc among states devoted to the cause of Christianity. No fair-minded person would be so foolish as to hold Christianity responsible for the wars of Europe or to argue that, as a religious doctrine, it breeds the plague of war. All are aware that the Western world has been the stronghold not only of Christianity but also of the nation-state, nationalism, industrial expansion, and a technology able to support national ambitions abroad with coercive power. What can be fairly alleged against the Christian nations is their failure to take their religion seriously enough to prevent the warlike tendencies peculiar to them from gaining the upper hand. Christianity never prevented the Western nations from coveting the lands of their neighbors, destroying one another to get advantages for themselves, or engaging in foul play and trickery in order to carry a ruthless system of imperialism to the uttermost corners of the globe. It never taught its followers to discard the prejudices of nationalism, nor to assume the responsibilities which go with power. Quite understandably the Amsterdam Assembly of the World Council in 1948 acknowledged, "The churches are guilty both of indifference and of failure"; desiring a higher standard of international conduct, the Assembly Report went on to say that the churches "cannot cast a first stone or excuse themselves for complacency." Today the churches are determined to make amends for their failure to win for Christianity a vital place in the relations of nations. They are determined that the nations of the Western world shall not behave like pagans.

The propriety of the decision of the churches to concern themselves with world affairs is, I believe, both clear and convincing. What is more, the churches have a genuine contribution to make toward a more stable order if, as most of us feel, Christianity can be related to the day-to-day activities of life. The question which I am raising in this discussion is whether the present methods of the churches are or can be made effective. By their present activities are the churches serving the cause which they have espoused or are they only meddling? Evidence can be adduced to show that, excellent as their motives may be, they often do more harm than good. In my opinion, churches should undertake a reappraisal of their policies, however agonizing the task may be.

II

Trial and Error (1918–1939)

Prior to 1914 the Protestant churches were not organized for institutional action on world problems, and, as earlier explained, individual clergymen were responsible for any attitudes asserted as Christian. Exercising their right to speak freely, clergymen gave their views on such subjects as the war with Mexico in 1846–1848, Spanish cruelties in Cuba in the 1890's, and the war of 1898 with Spain. It was clerical opinion, for instance, which the historian Mr. R. E. Osgood referred to when he wrote in regard to the war of 1898, "If any interest group, aside from the Navy, can be singled out for its special enthusiasm for going forth to battle, it is Protestantism, which was deeply impressed by Spanish inhumanity and its opportunities for missionary activity in the Orient."

The Federal Council of the Churches of Christ in America was created in 1908, but not until 1914 and World War I did the Commission on International Justice begin to function. It was also in 1914 that the Church Peace Union and the World Alliance for International Friendship Through the Churches began to work. None of the individual Protestant denominations set up an agency for the promotion of world peace until after World War I, although it was always possible for them to assert points of view through their separate national conventions.

On the first Monday after the United States broke off diplomatic relations with Germany early in February, 1917, the newspapers reported many Sunday sermons advocating that this country enter the war. President Wilson, still unwilling to take the fateful step,

remarked at that time, "I think our clergy have all gone crazy."
After the American declaration of war on April 6, all of the major
denominations supported the war effort vigorously, taking over
the prevalent doctrine that God was on the side of the Allies, while
the Devil was working through the Kaiser and his "Huns." Even the
Southern Baptists, critical as they were of the religious policies
of the War Department among our troops, found no fault with the
war effort in principle. Although the statement by Mr. Lloyd
George, a Baptist, soon after the Armistice that "the great war was,
at the bottom, for Baptist principles" would today provoke a knowing smile, in those days it sounded good, at least to Baptists; and
the members of other denominations would have felt equally com-
plimented had the remark equated the war objectives with their
principles. In behalf of church leaders, it must be said that their
simple assessment of right and wrong in those days was no different
from that of Americans everywhere. We were all new to world
politics and naïve in our estimates of the war aims of the belligerents and of the coming issues of peace. Christian leaders were no
more blind than were other Americans; but neither did they give
evidence of any special aptitude for handling international problems.

After the war, as unsettled controversies and conflicts piled up
and disillusionment began to set in, many church leaders regretted
their hasty analysis of wartime issues and aims, and with admirable
honesty said so. As was natural, a considerable number of them
went to a new extreme and announced an unqualified disapproval
of all war. Typical was the statement by the Chicago Federation
of Churches, representing 650 churches and fifteen denominations,
to the effect that, "In humble penitence for past mistakes and
sincere repentance for our want of faith and devotion to the ideals
of the Kingdom of God . . . we declare ourselves as unalterably
opposed to war." Somewhat similar was the assertion of General
Secretary Samuel McCrea Cavert of the Federal Council of
Churches: "I am disillusioned as to the causes of war. . . . I have
come slowly but clearly to the conclusion that the Church, in its
official capacity, should never again give its sanction to war or
attempt to make war appear holy."

With the war at an end, the churches began a campaign for peace, acknowledging, as the Universal Christian Conference on Life and Work (Stockholm, 1925) put it, "Christian repentance over the international disorder reflected in the War and its aftermath." Rather impulsively, in their quest for peace, the churches went into the business of foreign policy making. No major issue of policy came up in the 1920's or in the 1930's that did not evoke a stand of some kind by church authorities.

During this interval of two decades the churches worked individually through their own separate denominational bodies and collectively through the Federal Council of Churches. They made pronouncements on current issues, dispatched letters and petitions to the President and to congressmen, set up study groups and institutes, circularized the clergy and the laity, issued pamphlet material, published articles on international affairs in their religious journals, brought into their meetings speakers on foreign affairs, set aside designated Sundays to concentrate on some immediate objective such as disarmament, and on occasions sent representatives to testify before congressional committees. No one in touch with these activities, as many of us were in one capacity or another, could doubt the good will and sincerity behind them. Rarely, however, was it possible to identify the other qualifications which should characterize those who presume to say what American foreign policies ought to be. Lacking almost entirely in church positions on the concrete issues of policy was any evidence of familiarity with the realities of world politics or of a guiding philosophy of international relations. The churches wanted peace and justice, all of which was commendable, but they had little sense of direction. Both in strategy and in tactics they bungled. When at times they got what they wanted, they discovered later that what they had wanted was not worth the effort, and new disillusionment followed. On other occasions where the good and the evil did not stand out clearly for all to see—not an unusual condition—religious leaders would disagree and their voices canceled out each other. Always their approach was ethical; economics, history, law, and power politics had little place in their calculations.

The first great cause espoused by the churches after World War

I was the League of Nations. Except for the Southern Baptists and the Lutheran groups, all of the major Protestant churches of America announced through their respective national organizations their determination to support the Wilsonian project; they sent words of encouragement to President Wilson and a shower of telegrams to the Senate Foreign Relations Committee and to individual senators. Typical of their stand was the statement adopted by the Board of Bishops of the Methodist Episcopal Church in 1919 that "the League of Nations is an advance toward the period prophesied by the Hebrew prophet when men should not 'learn war any more.' " The editor of the *Christian Century*, Mr. Charles C. Morrison, looked upon the League as "the one saving feature of the Treaty." The Executive Committee of the Federal Council of Churches cabled President Wilson at Paris that the League is "the political expression of the Kingdom of God on earth."

After the defeat of the League by the Senate, the churches gave it very little attention and their interest in its work gradually decreased. True, on January 13, 1926, representatives of several church bodies met with a group of senators to urge support for the League; and from time to time utterances in its behalf were made. By the middle of the 1930's, however, after the Geneva organization had been defied by Japan in Manchuria, and its Disarmament Conference at Geneva in 1932–1933 had come to naught, many churchmen had become skeptical of the organization. For instance, in 1935 the Congregational-Christian churches polled about one-fourth of their members and found 90,000 against joining the League of Nations and only 60,000 in favor. Where were the churches right: in their enthusiasm for the League in 1918–1920, or in their indifference of the mid-thirties?

Early in 1921, with the League of Nations out of contention, the churches' efforts for peace centered on disarmament. Religious journals like *The Churchman*, *The Lutheran*, and *The Reformed Church Messenger* placed before their readers articles and editorials on the subject. Resolutions were adopted by church bodies embodying the theme expressed by the Northern Baptist Convention that "preparation for war is a cause of war." The Federal Council of Churches, the National Catholic Welfare Council, the Central

Conference of American Rabbis and the United Synagogue of America circularized 100,000 clergymen asking them to inform their congregations of the need for disarmament. The Church Peace Union sponsored and sent to President Harding a petition signed by 20,503 Protestant ministers, Catholic priests, and Jewish rabbis. In its report published in the *Yearbook of the Churches* for 1923, the Federal Council of Churches said that 500,000 copies of pamphlets had been distributed on disarmament, and claimed that out of nearly 14,000,000 letters received by the Advisory Committee of the Washington Conference on the Limitation of Armament, about 12,000,000 showed "evidence of having come from those who were thinking of the question in religious terms."

The Washington Conference on the Limitation of Armament was held in 1921–1922 and fixed limits in total tonnage for the capital ships and aircraft carriers of the United States, Great Britain, Japan, France, and Italy. In 1930 another conference, held at London, fixed similar limits for cruisers, destroyers, and submarines. A few years later the Nazis under Hitler began to threaten the peace of the world. At about the same time, Japan extricated herself from earlier agreements limiting her navy, and went into armament building in a big way. When World War II broke out in September, 1939, thoughtful people wondered whether the disarmament conferences at Washington and London had been realistic. Had they helped to set the stage for the aggression of the Axis powers? Had church enthusiasm for disarmament been misplaced?

No church venture of the interwar period was more in the spotlight than that in behalf of the Kellogg-Briand Pact of 1928 for the outlawry of war as an instrument of national policy. The churches began their campaign to make war illegal as early as 1923. Then in 1927 when Foreign Minister Briand of France proposed to the United States a bilateral treaty renouncing war between the two countries, the Federal Council of Churches became one of the first agencies to urge public support for the idea. The Department of State had Briand's note early in April, 1927, but had given little serious attention to it. The churches were in the forefront of the popular movement that led our government to resuscitate the Briand project and expand it to become a multinational renunciation of war as an instrument of national policy. The prominence of the churches in the movement which led to the final signature of the Pact on August 27, 1928, in Paris was well pointed up by Mr. Morrison of the *Christian Century* in an editorial of January 24, 1929, where he said, "It was the readers of the *Christian Century* who made the outlawry of war a reality."

Religious and secular reaction to the "Pact of Paris," as it came to be known, was jubilant. American naïveté in world affairs showed up at its worst. Only a few chronic doubters refused to go along with the general conviction that at last the planet had entered an era of permanent peace. Those of us whose memories reach back to that time will recall the cold stares which greeted the rare speaker, perhaps one in a dozen, who explained to his audience that the substance of world politics had in no way been changed by the Pact and that the causes of war were as much alive as ever.

Events of the 1930's showed the futility of the Pact of Paris as a war deterrent. Nations clashed on the field of battle and, to avoid charges that they had violated the Pact, they simply did not declare war or admit its existence. Japan invaded Manchuria in 1931; she launched a grandiose effort to conquer China in 1937, which she designated the "Chinese Incident." Italy invaded Ethiopia in 1935, and on this occasion the League of Nations held that war existed, although the aggressor had carefully avoided a declaration. Recurring battles were fought by Japanese and Russian troops along the Manchurian boundary with Siberia in the late 1930's without an admission of a state of war.

Only twice has the Pact of Paris played a prominent part in world affairs and on neither occasion was the result significant to the development of a peaceful world order. It was the basis of the Stimson Doctrine of 1932 which asserted that the United States would not recognize any territorial acquisition made by Japan or by any nation in violation of the Pact's renunciation of war as an instrument of national policy; this announcement neither coerced nor scared Japan into withdrawing from the new state of Manchukuo which she had set up on the soil of conquered Manchuria. More recently the Pact was heavily relied upon in the war-crimes trials of Germans and Japanese charged with bringing on World War II by open acts of aggression which amounted to the employment of war as an instrument of policy. Whether the trials were in fact legally justified by the Pact of Paris may long remain a moot question; but that they did little or nothing to ensure a stable and peaceful world is by this time obvious from the conflicts waged in Korea, Indo-China, the Middle East and elsewhere. It is in any case apparent that only the leaders of defeated nations will ever be obliged to stand trial; the warning, therefore, is not directed against war-makers but against war-losers.

The churches which had placed their enthusiastic support behind the Pact of Paris learned that a brief treaty of three vague articles condemning war was little more than preachment; it could not cleanse the hearts of nations nor contain their explosive policies. This learning was bought at a high cost in disillusionment and disappointment. The churches had given their best to what seemed to them a noble project, only to find that its substance was not gold but straw.

Signal good intentions continued to characterize the churches' efforts in foreign policy when, in 1931–1932, Japan sprung on the world a major crisis by her invasion of Manchuria. How should the United States meet this affront to world peace? Generally, the churches supported the Stimson Doctrine enunciated at that time, by which this country refused to recognize the new state of Manchukuo just set up by Japanese might. A poll taken among Protestant church members late in 1931, and reported by the *Literary Digest* on December 5, revealed a strong desire to supplement nonrecognition with an embargo on loans and war supplies for Japan in cooperation with the League of Nations; equally insistent was the belief that American warships should be kept at a safe distance from the scene of action and refuse to be drawn into the conflict. Our government did not see fit to sponsor an embargo, fearing that pressure of any kind on Japan would give aid to the military clique there, which was already strong.

The Manchurian affair brought to the forefront a dilemma of United States policy in which many Americans, including most churchmen, were caught. We were shocked at the aggression of Japan and wanted to stop it, but we were without the means of doing so. Our armament was not imposing, especially after the treaty limitations imposed upon us by the treaties of 1922 and 1930. In a military way we were weak in 1931, and Japan knew it. Yet suddenly we needed armament if we were to speak out effectively against aggression. The churches, along with other groups in the nation, wanted the United States to follow a policy of opposition to aggression but they were unwilling to give our government the means of effecting that policy. They were engrossed with the ends of policy but indifferent to means; they wanted what strong national power could provide, but they did not want power. Lacking the usual form of national power, the military, the churches advocated what they hoped would be an acceptable substitute— an embargo on loans and war supplies. Being in the depths of an economic depression, this nation had no enthusiasm for measures that would require a further tightening of the belt. In any case the efficacy of such measures against an aggressor was entirely conjectural at that time; a few years later they were tried against Italy in Ethiopia, and then they proved to be irritating to the aggressor but totally unable to thwart his designs.

The churches had backed the cause of American membership in the World Court when that issue was before the Senate in 1926, but when it came up again in 1935 their support was considerably less vocal and less insistent. Representatives of the Federal Council of Churches testified in behalf of the project before the Senate Foreign Relations Committee, and the *Christian Century* editorialized on the subject, but the separate denominational bodies had little to say. Isolationist forces of all kinds bombarded the Senate in opposition to membership, and defeated the project. Apparently the controlling interest of the churches by this time was the Nye Committee in the Senate, which, after investigating the armaments industry, reported late in 1934 that American and foreign munitions makers had been linked together to increase the sale of their products by bribery, lobbying, and other methods.

The operations of the Nye Committee brought into bold relief that quality of American public thinking which so often demands simple and ready solutions to profound problems. To reduce the causes of war to one—the armament producers' lust for profits—

was an alluring proposition; it dispelled baffling complexities about war and left in their place an understandable simplicity. The churches took a keen interest in the proceedings of the Nye Committee. The *Christian Century* delegated a special reporter to cover the hearings, and at their conclusion it printed a twenty-one page summary of the proceedings which was widely circulated among the churches for study. On one occasion Senator Nye addressed a meeting of the Federal Council and thanked its members for their support. Several of the denominations adopted resolutions on the results of the hearings; the Northern Baptist Convention, for instance, sought "legislation that will take the private profit out of war."

Clearly the Nye Committee hearings could be justified as long as they were kept in a proper perspective and looked upon as the routine investigation that they were; they disclosed irregularities, it is true, but not enough to justify labeling the industry a warmonger, or even enough to differentiate it from other profit makers in war. In retrospect, the most depressing aspect of the hearings was the excesses of interest and reaction displayed by the American people. The churches did not remain apart from those excesses.

With the Nye hearings out of the way, the American public became absorbed in setting up a system of neutrality that would keep this nation out of the next war. Hitler had come into power in Germany in 1933, and the portents of another war in Europe began to darken the thoughts and spirits of men. Following the logic of Mr. Charles Warren, who had been in charge of the enforcement of our neutrality laws between 1914 and 1917 in the United States Department of Justice, Americans were inclined to believe that, if another war could not be prevented, then the next best thing would be to adopt a formula of neutrality which would keep this country from involvement. Mr. Warren had argued in a widely read article entitled "Troubles of a Neutral," published in *Foreign Affairs* for April, 1934, that to maintain American neutrality in a new war this country might well give up rights claimed in World War I. The idea appealed to peace-loving Americans, and, beginning in 1935, a series of neutrality laws was enacted by Congress, which in final form called for an embargo on arms to belligerents, cash-and-carry arrangements for the sale of other commodities, travel restrictions on Americans, and a few other less stringent precautionary measures.

The first reaction of the churches toward these legislative devices for keeping our nation out of Europe's next war was favorable. The Federal Council declared that "the United States should withhold aid from all belligerents in any conflict that might arise." After the enactment of the 1935 law the *Christian Century* asserted that a nation "has a right to stay neutral at whatever cost, and that no cost which protects peace is too high." Similar pronouncements came from most of the individual denominations.

By 1937 the churches were less sure of how the United States should meet the impending crisis in Europe. By this time Germany had occupied the Rhineland contrary to treaty obligations, repudiated the war-guilt clause of the Treaty of Versailles, stepped up her rearmament program in earnest, and was persecuting the Jews disgracefully. On the other side of the world, Japan had launched on July 7, 1937, the "Chinese Incident." Shocking events like these stirred the moral indignation of many Christian leaders, who began to plead for the espousal of the cause of the weak against the cruel aggressors. In an article to the *Christian Century* of September 29, Dr. Reinhold Niebuhr said that America could stand by neutrality "only if we believe that peace is always preferable to the exploitation of the weak by the strong"; he believed that neutrality in the face of a clear issue of right and wrong would be "selfish isolationism." With other prominent churchmen swinging over to this point of view, it was not surprising that church groups found themselves in strong disagreement as to the course which a Christian should follow.

The National Peace Conference, headed in 1937 by Dr. Walter Van Kirk, discussed the Japanese aggression in China and announced that its participants had been unable to agree upon a recommendation for a Far Eastern policy for the United States. The World Alliance to Promote International Friendship Through the Churches had a similar experience. Referring to the failure of the churches to observe Armistice Day in the usual manner, Dr. Charles T. Holman of Chicago opined that "this perhaps reflects the confusion and division of counsel" of Christian leaders. The Presbyterian General Assembly which met in 1938 admitted that "people differ as to the best means of achieving this end [peace]." The Council for Social Action of the Congregational and Christian Churches debated the problem with the same inconclusive results. The churches harbored all shades of opinion, from those who would have peace at any price to those who would blockade Japan even if such action were to result in war.

The pacifist element within the churches diminished as the Nazi design for conquest became more apparent. The bloodless subjugation of Austria (March, 1938), the Munich fiasco (September, 1938) by which Germany obtained the Sudetenland, the extension of Nazi "protection" to all of Czechoslovakia (March, 1939), German pressure on Poland (spring and summer of 1939), and the announcement (August 23, 1939) of the German Nonaggression Pact with Russia which precipitated World War II—all won converts within the ranks of Christendom for a strong American policy of support to what seemed to be the cause of decency.

In the "great debate" of 1939–1941 between the "interventionists" and the noninterventionists, who were usually called "isolationists," the Christian counsel on American policy continued to be divided. In some instances the debate within the churches took on inordinate proportions. The ministers of many a church were roundly criticized for their interventionist or isolationist leanings, and sometimes were asked to resign.

As this brief survey of the twenty-year period discloses, we Americans, both in and out of the churches, were ill fitted for the role of world leadership that had been thrust upon us. We were new to the ways of world politics, most of us unaware of the manner in which the great nations—Germany, France, Italy, Japan, Russia, and Great Britain—had striven among themselves for power, some of them for centuries, to be used in a bitter competition of interests. In our forthright way, the majority of us assumed that other nations were, or at any rate should be, as satisfied with their lot in life as we were, and as free from guile. As the 1930's wore on and the aggressions of Germany, Japan, and Italy forced us into a closer observation of the details of international life, more Americans became aware of the reality of power politics and tried to think their way to tenable points of view toward it. Within the churches, Dr. Reinhold Niebuhr was a leader in this new approach, and, whether or not the readers of his books and articles agreed with his conclusions, they could not fail to admire his insistence that the facts of life be faced.

Some clergymen in the 1930's thought they observed in international relations little or nothing but a scramble for economic advantage. They were intrigued by the differentiation made by the journalist Mr. Frank Simonds between the "Have" and the "Have-not" nations, later picked up and emphasized by Hitler and other Axis leaders as an argument for a redistribution of the world's land resources. With World War II imminent in 1939, Dr. A. W. Palmer, president of Chicago Theological Seminary, and several other clergymen sent a letter to President Roosevelt asking for an economic conference to settle outstanding problems. The President gave audience to forty-five ministers on the subject, but nothing more came out of the proposal. What these men overlooked was the fact that the economic strife of the 1930's was in reality only a phase of the larger strife of power politics; nations sought economic advantages less for the actual profits which might accrue than for the strength made available for war. Economic self-sufficiency, or autarchy, was the goal of Germany and Italy because the possession within their boundaries of needed commodities would enable them in time of war to withstand a blockade and to produce for themselves the weapons and food required for a long fight. What the "Have-not" nations lacked was not so much a chance for a good livelihood through production and peaceful trade as it was an economy of power, capable of supporting a war effort.

The interwar period was further characterized in American thinking by a passion for panaceas. We went from one cure-all to another: the League of Nations; disarmament; the Pact of Paris; control of the munitions makers; and legislated neutrality. The churches for the most part followed along with this effort to reduce the complexities of world politics to something simple and manageable, only to meet with the frustration that all encountered. We should have known that anything which has persisted as doggedly as has war throughout recorded history must have many roots, all deeply embedded in our civilization.

All in all, the first period of church activity in international affairs, which began with World War I and ended with the opening of World War II, was not reassuring. Minor satisfaction might be found in the awakening of religious leaders to the need for improving the quality of American foreign policy and thus advancing the cause of peace. But the performance of those leaders raised serious doubt as to whether they had it in them to make any contribution. Like the rest of us, they inclined toward the superficial, ignoring the complexities of power politics and those underlying forces of international relations whose understanding must be the foundation of intelligent action. They knew that the world was in trouble, but they neither understood the reasons for its plight nor bothered to ascertain them. They felt that the churches had a duty to build a just and lasting peace, but, unskilled as they were in this type of construction work, they did not know what materials to use; methods and processes of building were equally alien to them. Consequently, whatever they built came falling down about as fast as it went up.

III

Old and New Methods (1939–1957)

The frustration which had beset Protestantism time and time again in 1919–1939 broke out anew when on September 1, 1939, Europe's armies began rolling. But, undaunted, its leaders continued their preoccupation with international problems both during and after World War II, convinced that "the churches and all Christian people have obligations in the face of international disorder," as the Amsterdam Assembly of the World Council of Churches declared in 1948.

At the outbreak of World War II, Dr. Buttrick, speaking for the Federal Council of Churches, made a radio plea for neutrality "from high and sacrificial motives, not for physical safety. . . ." In the "great debate" which engrossed the country during the two years preceding the Pearl Harbor disaster, exponents of neutrality, called "isolationists," were strong and vocal within the churches, but they encountered an ever growing group of "interventionists." Typical of the persistent swing toward giving aid to the nations fighting the Axis countries was a statement made in New York City on January 5, 1940, by twenty-seven Protestant leaders that a German victory would menace the "interests and ideals of the United States"; it urged that we enlist our "moral and material resources" to support the Allies. In November, 1941, some of the delegates to the World Alliance for International Friendship Through the Churches displayed impressive international sentiment, not advocating recourse to arms, but not condemning it either.

American entry into World War II was accepted by the churches, but with much less enthusiasm for a holy war than they had shown in 1917. Whereas in 1917 the great majority of the clergy looked upon the war as a crusade for right and justice, in 1941 there was more division among church leaders and less certainty of the course that a Christian ought to follow. Nothing showed this better than the meeting of the Federal Council of Churches in New York on January 5, 1942, when a day-long debate revealed strong contingents with divergent points of view, all the way from pacifists to holy-war advocates. The "Message to the Churches" adopted unanimously by the eighty members of the Council by-passed those differences, asserting that the church "honors the sincere conscience of every man." The members of the Council were in agreement on less controversial matters—their condemnation of the "recent aggression," their penitent admission of a "share in the events . . . which made it possible for these evil forces to be released," and their desire to "bring guidance to the perplexed" and to minister to our soldiers during the conflict.

During the war, the churches were among the first to give attention to the postwar problem of establishing and maintaining a lasting peace. As early as 1940, the Federal Council had at work its Commission to Study the Bases of a Just and Durable Peace. This Commission enlisted the services of men of first-rate talent, not the least of whom was Mr. John Foster Dulles, its chairman. Its studies embraced a wide range of subjects—international trade, territorial issues, colonial problems, a new world organization, and so on. A phase of this movement was the three-day conference of three hundred delegates from twenty-six denominations held at Delaware, Ohio, early in March, 1942, to consider the bases of an enduring peace. This effort of the churches, which continued throughout the war, remains one of the bright spots in the movement within Protestantism for world peace. It called forth the serious study of a considerable group of clergymen and laymen. Furthermore, the study and the reports put out were restricted to the fundamentals of international relations and did not presume to lay down the law on contemporary issues of policy, thus keeping the churches within an area where they can work effectively. No means are available for measuring the effects of this effort, the number of people whose thinking was affected, or the depth of whatever influence may have been exercised. From my own observations, I would say that only a small percentage of the leaders and laymen of the churches were reached in any substantial way, but that some few for the first time got an inkling of the complications of international relations and learned how to approach them intelligently. Even this was a significant accomplishment.

After World War II, the churches once again began emphasizing concrete issues of foreign policy; pronouncements emanated from city, state, national, and international meetings of denominational or interdenominational groups. On the national, interdenominational front the "Federal Council of Churches" was replaced by the "National Council of Churches" on January 1, 1951, the new body representing at that time twenty-nine denominations with nearly 34,000,000 members.[1] On the international, interdenominational front the new World Council of Churches and its Commission of the Churches on International Affairs have appeared on the scene with new methods of action.[2]

The quality of the pronouncements that have been made by church bodies cannot at this date be accurately rated; we are too close to them in point of time to know for sure whether the policies and opinions expressed were wise or unwise. Were one to attempt to analyze those policies and opinions in the light of experience, some would inevitably appear to be sound and others unsound. Many among them have been identical with official policies, while others have clashed with the government. Little, if anything, in the way of originality in policy making by the churches can be spotted.

[1] Headquarters of the National Council of the Churches of Christ in the U.S.A. are now located at 297 Fourth Avenue, New York City.

[2] Headquarters of the World Council of Churches are at 156 Fifth Avenue, New York City. An office is also maintained at 17 Route de Malagnou, Geneva, Switzerland.

With unimpeachable consistency the churches have upheld the cause of the United Nations and what it stands for from its early formative period down to the present time. As already noted, the Federal Council of Churches became one of the first American bodies to plan for a new world organization when in 1940 it set up a Commission to Study the Bases of a Just and Durable Peace. By 1943 this Commission had agreed on "Six Pillars of Peace": (1) a United Nations with universal membership; (2) world agreement on economic policies; (3) procedures for considering the revision of troublesome treaties; (4) a régime for the supervision and extension of autonomy to dependent peoples; (5) religious and intellectual freedom for all; and (6) an informed and moral public opinion. These findings were circulated among and discussed by religious groups throughout the country. When, late in 1944, the Dumbarton Oaks project for a United Nations was released to the public, it, too, was studied by church organizations.

At the San Francisco Conference of 1945, where the United Nations Charter took on its final form, there were among the forty-two private organizations represented by unofficial observers, several of a religious nature. Most conspicuous among them were the Federal Council of Churches, the Church Peace Union, the Catholic Association for International Peace, the National Catholic Welfare Conference, and two Jewish agencies. These observers were given access occasionally to the American official delegation, and they were accorded every reasonable means for making their views known. Just how vital their ideas were in fashioning the articles of the Charter would be difficult to determine, for there were always secular groups and official delegates supporting the same proposals that the churches were advancing. In any case, it is possible to say that many of the projects which the churches underwrote found their way into the Charter, such as the human-rights provisions, the eventual freedom of colonial peoples, the progressive development of international law, and an easier system of amending the Charter than that first considered. Like others who were present at San Francisco, the churches lost out in their effort to prevent the adoption of the veto.

The churches were active in urging that the Senate consent to the ratification of the Charter. Within twenty-four hours after the signing of the Charter at San Francisco, the Executive Committee of the Federal Council of Churches issued this statement asking for speedy ratification: "The Charter offers mankind an important means for the advancement of a just and durable peace. . . . The churches have long held that nations can better serve God's purpose for the world as they are brought into organic relationship with one another for the common weal. The Charter signed at San Francisco makes a general advance toward this end." That this appeal had much to do with the favorable Senate vote of 89 to 2 is unlikely, however, for the temper of the nation had greatly changed since 1919 and was strongly behind the United Nations idea from the beginning.

Once the Charter was ratified and the United Nations brought into being, the churches immediately began to advocate strong backing by the people and by the government for the organization and its work. Resolutions to that effect continue to emanate from church bodies. For instance, a Protestant Episcopal meeting at San Francisco in October, 1949, adopted a resolution calling upon the government to make a maximum use of the organization; again, during the Middle Eastern and Hungarian crises in 1956, the House of Bishops urged that "with all its inadequacies and imperfections, we believe that Christians are called upon to give their support to the United Nations, the only semblance of world government we possess." In like manner the Amsterdam Assembly of the World Council in 1948 declared that the United Nations "deserves the support of Christians." In 1953 the Fourth National Study Conference of the Churches at Cleveland made a similar plea.

Many recommendations of church bodies have dealt with specific programs of the United Nations. The human-rights activities rather naturally elicit the interest of Christians and the blessing of the churches; in this connection, the failure of the United States to ratify the Genocide Convention has caused consternation and led to resolutions for favorable action. The technical assistance program of the United Nations has also been promoted on numerous occasions: the World Council of Churches on August 31, 1954 appealed to the churches "to bid their members recognize their political responsibilities, and also to ask Christian technicians and administrators to find a vocation in the service of U.N. agencies engaged in meeting the needs of economically and technically underdeveloped countries." United Nations sanctions in Korea to meet the Communist invasion brought forth numerous expressions of approval: the World Council of Churches on July 26, 1950, asserted, "We commend the United Nations, an instrument of world order, for its prompt decision to meet this aggression and for authorizing a police measure which every member should support." On August 2, 1950, the American Federal Council of Churches likewise lauded the United Nations for its "prompt and vigorous action" in Korea. Pacifist bodies within the churches, like the Fellowship of Reconciliation, took the opposite view and condemned the policy of meeting force with force. As the Korean struggle wore on, the churches, like other segments of our society, became increasingly weary of it, urging negotiations looking toward its end. In the spring of 1955 a number of religious groups, including the National Council of Churches, the Detroit Council of Churches, and others, urged a greater use of United Nations procedures to stop the fighting in the neighborhood of Formosa. United Nations measures in the Middle East and its resolutions on the Hungarian crisis in 1956 were widely approved by the churches.

Church enthusiasm for the United Nations was made abundantly clear on World Order Sunday, scheduled by the National Council for October 23, 1955, one day before the tenth birthday of the organization; sermons throughout the nation drew attention to the work of the U.N. and solicited the continued backing of Christian people. This determination to play up the U.N. is also apparent from the practice of the Church Commission on International Affairs of keeping in close touch with United Nations agencies at all times, even working behind the scenes for policies and programs deemed meritorious.

To their credit, the churches have been more realistic in their attitude toward the United Nations than they were toward the League of Nations in its earlier years. To be sure, right after the signing of the Charter at San Francisco, many Americans, both in and out of the churches, expected more from the organization than it was equipped to give, and they have suffered disillusionment; but for the most part the exuberant optimism with which the League was greeted has not been revived. Realizing the many weaknesses of the United Nations, some church groups have encouraged discussions of Charter revision, and others have interested themselves in plans for world federation.

The proceedings and reports of the Evanston Assembly of the World Council in 1954 reveal a completely realistic attitude toward the United Nations. The failures as well as the successes of the organization were pointed up. The Report of the Section on International Affairs lamented the veto of applications by states for membership in the U.N., the indifference of members to Charter commitments, and the evasion of the U.N. by unilateral action (earlier alleged by some groups to have occurred in the enunciation of the Truman Doctrine). A review conference was advocated ". . . to determine the organic and structural requirements of the U.N. for carrying out programs dealing with universal enforceable disarmament, human rights, greatly expanded technical assistance, and more rapid development of self-government in colonial areas."

Both inside and outside the United Nations, the churches have striven in their pronouncements and activities for a system of international control of atomic energy. They have been alive both to the disastrous potentialities and to the peacetime utility of the power wrapped up in the atom. As early as October, 1945, the Federal Council asked the United States Government to make the United Nations the medium for the construction of a control system equipped to prevent atomic warfare—a request which was unnecessary, for our government had decided to do so in any case. From this time on, the subject has never been neglected. Like national bodies, the World Council has advocated a ban on atomic and hydrogen weapons, and sought an adequate system of inspection and control.

The place of the military in international affairs has continued to baffle Christian leaders. Church manifestoes reveal less agreement on this subject than on any other. A halt to further armament building by the United States, both in nuclear and in conventional weapons, has been advocated not only by the more pacifist-inclined groups, such as the Quakers and the Church of the Brethren, but at times by others; multilateral, rather than unilateral, arms limitation has, however, been the more frequent approach of the major denominations. The Federal Council, late in 1945, urged the American delegation at the General Assembly of the United Nations to work toward multilateral action. Both the Amsterdam Assembly (1948) and the Evanston Assembly (1954) of the World Council asked for multilateral discussions of the control of nuclear weapons and the limitation of all armaments. In 1956 considerable support for a ban on the further testing of nuclear weapons was voiced by much the same church groups that had been vocal on the limitation of armaments.

Many sectors of Protestantism have continued to oppose compulsory military training in time of peace, whether in the form of conscription or universal military training. The subject was freely discussed in 1948, at which time Mr. Leyton Richards expressed in the *Christian Century* (September 1, 1948) a point of view widely held: peacetime conscription, he said, is "an ironical sequel to victory over military dictatorship"; and, he argued, "a potential enemy can always be found to justify . . . compulsory [military] training for war." In the same year three hundred clergymen called upon American youth to defy the new draft law; others denounced this appeal as disloyal. At the same time, a Kentucky Methodist Episcopal Conference at Richmond criticized those young men of their faith who were refusing to register for the draft, suggesting that they register and then claim exemption as conscientious objectors, according to law.

Universal military training was bitterly opposed by the National Council of Churches in 1952, and again in 1955. On January 13, 1955, President Eisenhower proposed universal military training to Congress along lines worked out by a special committee which he had appointed to study the question. Immediately a cry of alarm broke out in religious quarters. In an editorial (January 26) the *Christian Century* asserted that the project "would spread control by the Pentagon over more Americans at a younger age and for a longer period than ever, while there is no evidence as yet to suggest that it would provide effective military units." Methodist Episcopal Church Boards then in session at Cincinnati adopted resolutions against the plan. Meeting at Columbus, Protestant pastors of Ohio took similar action, and elsewhere in the country church groups argued against the project. The National Council of Churches took up the issue in March and found that its 244 members present were divided, with a slight majority against U.M.T. When the bill in Congress came up for a hearing, spokesmen of several religious bodies, including the National Council, the Presbyterian Church in the U.S.A., the Methodist Episcopal Church, and the Disciples of Christ appeared in committee against it.

The churches have been far from unanimous in their attitude toward American security pacts—NATO, SEATO, and the others. When the North Atlantic Treaty was under consideration in 1948 the *Christian Century* was particularly critical of it, believing it to be "hollow and deceptive," a "step toward war" and a means of "alienating the confidence of the European masses." In December, 1949, after the Treaty had been in effect for several months the Federal Council expressed its opposition to alliances. On the other hand, the Section on International Affairs at the Evanston Assembly maintained that "regional groupings" of this nature "have a valid place in a cooperative world order, provided: (1) they are clearly defensive in character and military actions are subject to collective decision; (2) they are subordinate to and reinforce the aims of the Charter of the United Nations; (3) they serve the genuine mutual interests and the needs of the peoples of the region."

Technical assistance and economic aid, as policies of the United States Government, have made a strong appeal to churchmen. Many statements have been made in favor of helping underdeveloped nations by these devices. The churches have opposed cutting down congressional appropriations for such purposes, and they have advocated divorcing all programs from military policies. Typical was the statement of Christian Action (an interdenominational social action group) in 1955 that technical assistance is a means "of giving substance to our nation's deep religious roots."

Another issue which has figured prominently in church discussions since World War II has been that of dispatching a diplomatic envoy to the Vatican. Protestantism has strongly contended against the idea. Prior to the 1948 presidential election, *Missions*, a Baptist publication, sent inquiries to the candidates asking how they stood on the subject, and was widely commended for doing so. State and national denominational bodies have voiced their opposition from time to time, and in 1951–1952 the National Council of Churches carried on a campaign against the appointment of an ambassador. The influential *Christian Century* has devoted its energy to the same end. On few issues have Protestant spokesmen been in such general agreement.

To the above subjects of church pronouncements, others may be added which less frequently or in a less general way provoked statements of policy attitudes. Although not presented as a complete list, the following points of view have been asserted by one or more religious groups and have had a measure of national publicity:

(1) opposition to the proposed agreement with Spain in 1955 to provide the United States with military bases;

(2) opposition to American withdrawal from the United Nations, if the Peiping government were given the Chinese seat in the organization;

(3) opposition to the proposed Bricker amendment to the Constitution, aimed at changing the treaty-making powers of our government;

(4) approval of an expanded world trade;

(5) opposition to economic aid to fascist Spain;

(6) opposition to colonialism;

(7) criticism of the war-crimes trials;

(8) criticism of the Truman Doctrine of 1947;

(9) approval of the admission of Red China to the United Nations;

(10) desire for a stronger system of international law;

(11) desire for giving further assistance to refugees;

(12) desire for an enlarged program of economic and technical aid abroad.

By far the most significant organizational developments of the churches in international affairs since World War II have been the reorganization of the World Council of Churches and the creation of the Commission of the Churches on International Affairs. Although the World Council had been functioning for some time, it did not come formally into being until August 23, 1948, when the Amsterdam Assembly drafted a constitution setting it up as a permanent organization. The Assembly of delegates of the churches from many different countries is the basic deliberative body of the organization.

In addition to its Assembly, which will meet every few years, the organization of the World Council of Churches includes (1) a six-member presidium chosen by the Assembly, (2) a ninety-member Central Committee, also elected by the Assembly, (3) an executive committee composed of the six presidents who constitute the presidium, the two chairmen of the Central Committee, and twelve other members chosen from the Central Committee, and (4) a Secretariat; these are permanent bodies, able to function when the Assembly is not in session. The Secretariat, which includes from forty to fifty staff members, maintains offices in New York City and in Geneva, Switzerland.

Although the World Council promotes cooperation in many lines of endeavor, in none has its work attracted more attention than in international relations. I have already alluded to the work of Section IV on International Affairs of the Amsterdam and Evanston assemblies. Even more significant, however, has been the activity of the Commission of the Churches on International Affairs (C.C.I.A.), established in 1946.

The C.C.I.A. represents a new approach by the churches to world problems. It is founded upon the assumption that there are aspects of international affairs which can be more effectively handled by an ecumenical agency than by national or local bodies. The activities of such agencies as the National Council of Churches in the United States, local councils, and denominational organs go

on much as before; their work is not terminated, but rather supple-
mented, by that of the C.C.I.A. As a denationalized, or perhaps I
should say multinationalized, body, the C.C.I.A. is believed to be
particularly qualified to speak with authority on questions arising
within the United Nations. Even on issues of national policy its
recommendations to governments are presented with the hope that
they will seem politically detached, as well as Christian, in substance.

Another advantage claimed for the C.C.I.A. as a vehicle of
Christian opinion is its permanent availability, as contrasted with
national, local, or denominational bodies, whose meetings are in-
frequent. Furthermore, it can dispatch a member to any troublesome spot on the earth's surface with recommendations for
improved relations, as in 1953 Mr. O. F. Nolde, Director of the
Committee, was sent to Korea to tell President Rhee of the Christian hope for a restoration of peace in that country.

The advantage most frequently urged for the C.C.I.A is that it
contains a nucleus of men continually at work on world problems
and therefore informed and able to speak authoritatively. The
quality of church activities, so it is hoped, will reflect this pro-
ficiency. In place of the off-the-cuff opinions which have often
characterized the stands of churchmen on world problems, so the
reasoning goes, there will be well-considered points of view.

According to Mr. O. F. Nolde, the work of the C.C.I.A. is
based upon the following principles:

"(1) The Christian message has meaning for relations between
peoples and nations as well as individuals, but without technical skill and hard study, this message cannot be understood and carried out.

(2) Resolutions and statements by church agencies may have
general educational value, but they have political effect
only if their influence is felt at the time and place where
decisions of international political importance are reached.

(3) Periodic conferences are helpful in shaping policies, but
. . . there must be programs which can function virtually
every day of the year.

(4) World-wide Christian fellowship needs an organization for harnessing its resources. . . .

(5) There is a need for such contacts with international governmental bodies as will permit a Christian voice to be raised, but at all costs the Church must avoid any political or economic entanglements which would compromise the principles of their faith."

According to a news story in the *Christian Century* (June 2, 1954) the C.C.I.A. is in a position to make assessments "of political realities and of Christian opinion." It is able to approach "political leaders directly to acquaint them with the churches' attitudes on international affairs." As the article further asserts, it "constitutes a sounding board and a policy-making body on behalf of the churches."

In its work the C.C.I.A. reaches out in two directions. First, because it is a spokesman for the churches it maintains contact with national church bodies in order to know their thinking and thus to be able to represent their views more effectively. For instance, when early in 1953 the C.C.I.A. was endeavoring to prevent the Korean conflict from spreading, it worked closely with national councils and departments. To deal with the problem of Arab refugees a few years ago, the C.C.I.A. first called a conference in Beirut to discuss the subject; the findings of the conference were then sent to national departments and councils. Prior to the General Assembly sessions of the United Nations, national groups have often met, discussed issues, and sent their opinions to the C.C.I.A. to help guide that agency in its efforts to influence action.

The C.C.I.A., in its activities, also establishes contacts with governments and with the United Nations. Once convinced that a given course of action is wise, the C.C.I.A. will either apprise the governments concerned of their views or they will ask national councils or departments to do so. If the subject be one within the purview of the United Nations, contact will be made with delegates of the nations to the General Assembly, the Security Council, or whatever organ is dealing with it. Staff members of the Committee have been present at all General Assembly sessions in recent years and at many of the other meetings held within the United Nations.

For the most part, therefore, the C.C.I.A. operates behind the scenes, trying to influence officials of governments and leaders of the United Nations into its way of thinking.

The C.C.I.A.'s activities will, of course, take on whatever form commends itself in a given situation. In February, 1955, with the authorization of the World Council's executive committee, it called a meeting at Geneva, Switzerland, of representative churchmen from the western European states to deliberate on the subject of German rearmament in general and the new Paris agreement in particular. Reference has been made already to the practice of the director to visit personally an area of international tension. To strengthen church understanding and guidance in international affairs, the Committee helps prepare Assembly meetings of the World Council; months before the Evanston Assembly convened, it decided upon the issues to be emphasized in Section IV and got together working papers and drafts of proposals for consideration.

During its rather short lifetime the C.C.I.A. has dealt with a variety of problems both inside and outside the United Nations: the Korean conflict, the repatriation of prisoners, technical assistance, the race problem in South Africa, the Arab-Israeli controversy, human rights, religious freedom, and many others. In doing so, it has attempted to adjust its methods both to what it considers to be the opinions of its constituent churches and to the nature of the problem. Mr. Werner Kägi has explained this attempted adjustment in the following way:

(1) where there is "fundamental agreement, approaching complete understanding," in the attitudes of constituents, the common point of view is forthwith presented to the governments and international organs concerned;

(2) where there is obvious disagreement, then "a clear, open statement of the opposing views" is given to the authorities with the hope that it will prove helpful;

(3) where there are important church groups in two contending countries, an effort is made to render a service by "bringing greater objectivity to bear on the judgment and settlement of the conflict";

(4) where two or more governments "are trying to achieve a

common policy on a certain question, then the churches
must try to influence . . . their countries in the direction of
this agreement";

(5) where human rights, especially religious liberty, have been
infringed, "the C.C.I.A. has tried to remove these restrictions through consultation with the governments involved,
through the communication of factual information, and if
necessary through publicity";

(6) church representatives "have from time to time participated
directly in intergovernmental negotiations";

(7) "continuing influence" has been exerted on the work of the
United Nations and its specialized agencies.

Looking back on church activities and methods since World War
II, the observer asks himself the question: do they represent improvement? Have the churches made themselves more effective
than they were in the 1920's and 1930's? Are the United States
and the world better off than they would have been without the
participation of the churches in international politics?

As one tries to think through such questions as these, he immediately reflects on the crises and tensions which have harassed
the world since World War II; rarely has there been so much
hostility in time of "peace" among nations. To chide the churches,
or even our government, for a failure to turn these dark years into
a period of sweetness and light would be an impertinence, for the
cause of most of the trouble has been centered outside our own
boundaries and within the Soviet Union. The churches have been
working in one of the most frustrating periods of world politics.
For a few years following the death of Stalin there was optimism in
some quarters that diplomacy might function in a clearer atmosphere, but Russian oppression in Hungary and intervention in the
Middle East in 1956 brought us back to a realization of the communists' unswerving loyalty to world revolution by all means available, decent or indecent.

Appraising the work of the churches, without going into the
details of their pronouncements, we may first observe that on the
major issue of security for the United States and other nations in

the face of communist aggressions, the churches have contributed little or nothing. They have shown a keen awareness of the problem and have made minor suggestions, like that favoring negotiations to end the Korean conflict, but nothing basic or significant for straightening out Soviet-American relations has been offered. In this respect the record of the churches is no better and no worse than that of other nongovernmental agencies. The enormity of the problem is sufficient reason why no one outside the government could hope to work out solutions. That even the government has made mistakes is not surprising.

If it be conceded that neither the churches nor any other private agency may be expected to come up with solutions to a problem as baffling as the East-West controversy, then what is the type of problem which nongovernmental groups can tackle successfully? Is not the logic of it all that *initiative* in foreign policy belongs with the government in all significant policy making? The main job of the public in our democracy is not to initiate, but to criticize, approve, or oppose. Indeed, not all elements of the public, not all organizations, are equipped even to perform these functions.

With the over-all policy objective of our government in East-West relationships—"containment," as it is called—the churches have been satisfied; they have not doubted the wisdom of trying to prevent further Russian expansion. The government's policies in furtherance of that objective frequently have met with approval but at times with sharp censure, usually from pacifist-inclined groups. The Marshall Plan for Europe was widely supported, usually with enthusiasm; the Point Four program has been uniformly welcomed by the churches; and what little has been said on the idea of western European unity by Christian leaders has been favorable. Pacifist criticism has been leveled mainly at the Truman Doctrine, the rearming of Germany, and our alliances. From these facts it is apparent that exercise by religious groups of their right to criticize has not resulted in any modification of governmental policy. Having taken no effective initiative and having failed to modify the course of governmental action by criticism, the churches have not contributed appreciably to the content of our policies toward the Soviet world. If they have been helpful at all, it has been by extending support, at times united and at times divided, to the efforts of the government.

On the other major issue since World War II—the problem of national self-determination in the colonial areas—evidence again is lacking of church influence on the content of American policy. Christian leaders have been sympathetic with the nationalistic aspirations of the peoples of Asia and Africa, and they have made pronouncements against colonialism. In doing so, they usually have neglected to consider that the military bases provided by the colonial areas to our allies, Great Britain and France, are one source of strength to us in our effort to contain the Soviet Union. Pursuing principle at any cost, they also disregard the fact that by supporting colonial peoples at this particular juncture in history we may lose our strongest NATO allies; should this happen we shall in all probability have opened the way for renewed Russian aggression and the enslavement of peoples now free. The great dilemma of recent American foreign policy the churches have rarely recognized and certainly never solved: if we support the empires of Great Britain and France, we lose the friendship of the Asian and African peoples; and if we support the independence movements of the Asian and African peoples we weaken our alliances, perhaps fatally. As our government has jumped from one horn of this dilemma to the other, trying to protect our interests everywhere, the churches have been inclined to perch on one horn—independence to the Asian and African people—quite oblivious to the other, and oblivious, too, to the fact that principle is involved in both cases; for certainly it is quite as wrong that the Soviet empire be extended as that the old empires continue to live.

Despite these shortcomings, one change which American Protestantism has undergone in the last fifteen or twenty years is a clearer understanding of power politics and, occasionally, a wider acceptance of it. The proper role of power in world affairs still remains, however, a debated subject in Christian circles, so that now as ever the churches are not always consistent. Speaking of the Berlin crisis, the *Christian Century* on July 21, 1948, declared, "Such a crisis as has suddenly developed in Berlin furnishes another sobering reminder of the danger of power politics." Yet when South

Korea was invaded, this journal thoroughly approved of the use of power against the aggressor, and almost all of the power employed was American.

Church pronouncements and activities indicate that the idealism of Christian leaders remains very much alive, despite their greater acceptance of power politics. Causes which look toward peace, such as the United Nations, have had a special appeal to them. When they espouse power in an international situation, they see in it an objective which they deem to be commendable, such as the halting of an aggressor or the protection of the weak.

The humanitarian emphasis of the churches in policy matters has continued throughout the postwar era, as they have sought to promote human rights and economic assistance. Whether government policy or United Nations programs have been modified by these activities is conjectural, for little but hearsay can be adduced in the way of evidence. In this connection, it is pertinent to bring out that the churches themselves have engaged in humanitarian work on an international basis. By way of illustration, in 1956 they sent relief supplies to victims of war in Hungary and in the Middle East through the National Council of Churches; at the same time, the president of the Council, Dr. Eugene Blake, cabled a message to the churches of the Soviet Union suggesting that they, too, send help.

What about the methods used by the churches since the war? On the national front, the old methods (pronouncements, letters or telegrams to public officials, study groups or conferences, the publication of literature, special Sundays devoted to designated causes, and so on) are still used much as during the interwar period. It is on the ecumenical front, represented by the World Council and its C.C.I.A., that new methods have been conspicuous.

Undoubtedly the methods of the C.C.I.A. have the advantages claimed for them earlier in this chapter—they reduce the element of national bias in favor of a broader international perspective, and they utilize the skill and knowledge of the few men who make up the Committee and its staff. The offsetting disadvantage of C.C.I.A. methods is that these few leaders will have too much control and their points of view will not accurately reflect the opinions of the churches for which they assume to speak. To be sure, the C.C.I.A. attempts to keep in touch with the churches and get their views, at least in so far as it is possible for a committee to maintain a close working relationship with large constituencies in many countries. That the Committee will have the views of national councils and departments, which in turn will be informed of Christian thinking by the denominations and local organizations within the separate nations, is an appealing theory of democracy, but can it be anything more than a theory? Does it work that way in fact? Few of the church members who sit in the pews on Sunday express views that travel on to the higher-ups, and few clergymen relay opinions to the higher echelons. Indeed, most of these people do not even know of the system of the C.C.I.A. At best, then, it all boils down to a few church leaders within various nations working with the Committee. These few can assume to state *a* Christian point of view, but they are in no position to express *the* Christian point of view. Can government officials or the United Nations get much help from one Christian viewpoint, knowing as they do that there may be and usually are other Christian attitudes on a given subject?

One of the accomplishments most frequently ascribed to the C.C.I.A. was its work for the creation of a system of observers for the United Nations in 1950, when the project known as "Uniting for Peace" was before the General Assembly. Because the purpose of "Uniting for Peace" was to define Assembly duties in the prevention and treatment of aggression, the C.C.I.A. took the position that it might well incorporate a plan for the dispatch of observers to an area of international tension to prevent open combat. In its final form "Uniting for Peace" included this suggestion. Just how influential the C.C.I.A. actually was in bringing about its adoption is debatable. The *New York Times* has contended that the idea did not originate in the C.C.I.A., as some churchmen have said, but in the Department of State. The *Christian Century* of August 30, 1950, maintained that the C.C.I.A. was a "stooge" of the United States Government in its advocacy of the plan. Doubt has been raised, too, as to whether the observer system will have practical utility; to date it has been used sparingly.

IV

A Man-Sized Job

No person with a background in foreign affairs or in the broader area of constructing a durable system of peace will underestimate the complexities encountered by men in high places within our government. Most Americans do not have such a background, and as a consequence their thinking runs the risk of immaturity, often hindering rather than helping the government. In the churches there is a nucleus of leaders both in this country and abroad who have been working in foreign affairs for many years and have learned in the school of hard knocks that it takes more than good will and lofty purposes, helpful as these can be, to advance the cause of peace. These leaders have in the past frequently benefited from the advice of laymen with diplomatic experience such as Mr. John Foster Dulles, presently Secretary of State, and Mr. Ernest Gross, formerly a United States ambassador to the United Nations. The great majority of churchmen are, however, like other Americans, amateurs in world affairs.

The purpose of this chapter is to recount some of the intricacies of foreign policy making and of the vast problem of peace with which the churches have been tangling for some four decades now. To do so may provide a clue to the proper role of religious groups and of the public generally in foreign affairs. In any case it should produce in us all the becoming modesty of William Penn in the opening words of his *An Essay Towards the Present and Future Peace of Europe* (1693): "I have undertaken a subject that, I am very sensible, requires one of more sufficiency than I am a master of to treat it as in truth it deserves and the groaning state of Europe calls for." Our encouragement perhaps is, like Penn's, that "bunglers may stumble upon the game as well as masters."

First to note is the elemental fact that the United States is but one of some ninety states inhabiting this planet, each pursuing its own separate policies and often willing to risk international friction, perhaps even war, to have its way in matters of vital importance. Moreover, a given nation may be wholly circumspect in every phase of its policy but still be plunged into crises and conflict by the recklessness of another. The job of diplomats is to reconcile the policies of these ninety states, a man-sized undertaking when all are cooperative, and one which is humanly impossible when any nation is recalcitrant. In 1938–1939 France and Great Britain were anxious for peace, and to keep it made extensive concessions in Austria and Czechoslovakia, but all in vain, for Germany and her Axis allies were bent on expansion, even at the high cost of war. Nowadays Russia wants a communist world and has nettled the free nations no end in her pursuit of that objective. In 1956 Egypt's ill-considered nationalization of the Suez Canal Company temporarily upset the delicate equilibrium which we call peace. Let us then begin by recognizing the complicated world into which our foreign policies must be fitted, and admit that trouble in international affairs is no proof that our government has been at fault. We suffer from the blunders of others as well as from our own.

To be sure, there are things which a great power like the United States can do to keep other nations from blundering or to prevent the dire effects from spreading like a forest fire until all are victimized. Perhaps it is true, as some believe, that had the United States not been lured by the dream of neutrality in the 1930's and had either hinted or warned that we would oppose Nazi aggression, no war would have occurred in 1939. Secretary Dulles believes that his threat of force kept Red China a few years back from becoming an active belligerent in Indo-China. Threats of this nature are commendable when they operate to prevent or to localize war, but they are disastrous when they do not, as in 1939

France and Great Britain threatened war on Germany if Poland were attacked, only to find that their ultimatums were not the deterrents they had hoped.

A great power indeed has other recourses than the threat of force in the effort to keep the world right side up. It may try persuasion and reason, with the hope of working out compromises. Using foresight, it may by its policy—foreign aid, for example— endeavor to prevent any deterioration in world conditions likely to lead to a crisis. In the long run, however, there is only so much which a peace-minded nation, such as we believe ourselves to be, can do to forestall misunderstanding and conflict.

Mr. C. B. Marshall, formerly of the Department of State, asserts that after a speech which he once gave to a Texas audience, a gentleman inquired as to whether or not the Department had foreseen the friction in North Africa between France and her dependencies. After receiving a "yes" to his query, the questioner followed up with, "Then why did you not prevent it?" Mr. Marshall uses this incident to bring out the limitations of our government in diplomacy; had it tried to prevent conflict between France and her dependencies, it would have been rightly accused of a type of intervention which no nation will tolerate. This tendency of Americans to expect their government to prevent all that is ill in international affairs, or to apply a magic cure should preventive measures somehow fail, is also brought out in our election campaigns. If there be civil strife in China, war in Korea, or unsolved problems in the Middle East at election time, the people are told that it is the party in power which is to be blamed; and most of us believe it, wholly indifferent to the mistakes of other nations whose actions our government cannot control. No wonder both Secretary of State Acheson and Secretary Dulles fell into wide popular disfavor, for they were expected to do the impossible and held to blame if by a quick flick of the finger they did not dispel the world's ills.

In another sense foreign policy making is today a global operation. No longer can the United States take an active interest in Latin America and remain "isolated" from Europe. Before 1850 we gave little attention to the Far East, except for trade purposes;

now that part of the world is so vital to our welfare that statesmen have argued among themselves as to whether our postwar emphasis upon European affairs was not made at the sacrifice of our Asian interests. Only a short time ago, the policy maker could virtually ignore Africa; but now the resources of that continent, its relation to the strategy of war, and its restless people demanding independence have forced it out of its traditional darkness into a blaze of light.

No longer can such a term as "Far Eastern policy" or "European policy" convey much sense. Nearly everything which we do in one part of the world has repercussions in every other part; and nearly everything that happens anywhere must have the attention of the Department of State. Quoting Mr. C. B. Marshall again, "The world tends to take on the character of a drum: agitated at any point on its surface, it resounds throughout." When the United States showers economic assistance on Europe or Asia, the Latin Americans get out of sorts, feeling that we are slighting them in their effort to improve their standards of living. If we support the independence of colonial peoples in Asia and Africa, we antagonize Great Britain, France, and Belgium, against whom the colonial peoples have been rebelling; if we support the European powers as allies of ours, we lose the friendship of the Asian and African natives. When it comes to the defense of South Korea, our government must beware lest it drain off the fighting strength of the NATO powers pledged to defend the Atlantic area. So the world looks to a diplomat like a teeter board: to force one end up is to push the other down. What American policy in a world of this kind will produce the general contentment and good will that must be the foundation of peace?

Perhaps nothing is more baffling in policy making than the unforeseen and the unforeseeable. If a trained statesman could sit down at his desk and list on a sheet of paper all of the facts and factors which both today and in the future will affect the policy he must make, it would be relatively simple. Even the policy maker in Washington cannot gather together all the facts he would need, despite his access to State Department documents and those of the Central Intelligence Agency. Without official status, we of the general public are in a position immeasurably weaker. Indeed, as Eleanor Dulles of the Department of State has brought out, ". . . many aspects of foreign relations are by their very nature obscure." They are, she said, ". . . to be compared to the iceberg which is visible only as a small portion appears above the surface of the water. However visible and clear this mass appears, the part which is not seen is many times as large." Professor Feliks Gross, who, in his *Foreign Policy Analysis*, has tried to reduce policy making in so far as possible to a science, also calls attention to the obscurities—the elements of chance, accident, and irrationality—which he labels "factor X."

That the unknown and the unknowable are always present to confound the diplomat is evident in the day-to-day events of international politics. No one could foresee, for instance, either the time of Stalin's death or the resulting change of face in Russian policies which would pose new and different problems to our government. That President Nasser in 1956 would lose his temper after the United States and Great Britain withdrew their offers of aid for the building of the Aswan Dam and nationalize the Suez Canal Company could not have been prophesied. Who can tell what the outcome of the next national elections in France will be or how it will affect French policy?

This unknown element in foreign affairs implies that the policy maker bent on peace can use rational processes only so far as his information goes; beyond that, he must do some guessing. If he guesses right, he is a great statesman; if he guesses wrong, woe be unto him! To pursue the analogy, the policy maker must take chances, much as a gambler does: if he wins, he is a hero, but if he loses, he is a rascal.

Complicating further the work of the policy maker in a democracy is his obligation to keep a watchful eye on public opinion. Even though he believes that he knows what should be done by his government, he will hesitate and perhaps reverse his decision if the public disagrees with him. As Mr. F. H. Russell, formerly of the State Department, once said, "Foreign policy in this country can never get very far ahead of or very far behind public opinion." Evidence has been adduced to show that President Roosevelt believed, whether he was right or wrong, that American welfare and interests were on the side of the democratic powers in World War II long before the people were ready to go along with a partisan policy. Mr. Walter Lippmann has pointed out that often in foreign affairs the people are several jumps behind the government in sizing up a situation and settling on a policy to meet it.

When the policy maker examines the opinion of the public which he must please he almost never finds any one point of view held unanimously by all, or even by all who have expressed themselves. Instead, he will find some people favoring one course of action, others advocating a different course, and perhaps a third group totally uncommitted. In 1939–1941, some Americans wanted to join with Britain and France in the war against the Axis aggressors; a second group desired complete neutrality; and a third were for keeping out of hostilities but extending to Britain and France all possible aid in defiance of the law of neutrality. In 1956, as our nation began reconsidering its policy of foreign aid, the fact became apparent that some among us wanted aid continued as before, some wanted it separated completely from military assistance abroad, some wanted it administered by the United Nations, while the largest group of all appeared indifferent. What, besides going mad, can a policy maker do in a situation like this?

Then the policy maker can never afford to ignore the Congress. The experience of President Wilson will remind him that, if his policy is in a treaty, he must be able to get two-thirds of the Senate behind him. If there is a treaty requiring the expenditure of money, or a policy like the Marshall Plan entailing an appropriation of many billions, he must consider the reactions of the House of Representatives as well as the Senate. Even when his own political party controls the Congress, he still must watch out, for party discipline in Congress is so weak that his political friends as well as his enemies can undo him. Should a presidential proposal come out of Congress in anything like the form in which it was submitted, our chief executive may consider himself in luck.

How do these observations on the difficulties of foreign policy making relate to the churches? As a portion of the American public, it is easy for us all, church members and others, to become irritated and impatient when trouble of any kind breaks out in international relations. Scanning events in retrospect and acting the part of a Monday-morning quarterback, we see, or think we see, where our government should have called a different play. We then jump to the conclusion that our government does not know its business in foreign affairs, and that we, with our superb hindsight, must somehow take over the job of policy making. The clergy, as much as any sector of the American public, need to be warned against underestimating the immensity of the problems faced by the government in making foreign policy and against the temptation to offer ready, often ill-considered, solutions.

Exasperated with the baffling problem of finding policies which, in harmony with those of other nations, will set up a durable peace, many Americans have concluded that a new world order must be created—perhaps world federation or, as a starter, a federation of the democracies. The present order, in which ninety nation-states, all sovereign, endeavor to promote their separate policies in disregard of others and at the same time to avoid conflict through procedures of cooperation and conciliation, has been made to seem unreal and inadequate by modern science, which ties men of all nations inextricably into "one world," as Wendell Willkie called it after his globe-circling trip. This project of reform is one with a special appeal to Christian leaders, motivated as they are and as they should be, by the idealism of their faith.

The problem of peace is altered but not simplified by this shift away from a search for sound national foreign policies within our present international society to a quest for a new world order. All of the logic, to be sure, is in favor of a new order, but everything else pulls for the status quo. Few will deny in point of logic that our present system of nation-states is inadequate to our needs, that such problems as health, traffic in opium, trade, crime, and travel require a world-wide rather than a national approach. The airplane, to give us a maximum of service, must be freed from the doctrine of national sovereignty and be allowed to fly unrestricted wherever it can be beneficial to mankind, whether over the territory of the United States or that of the Soviet Union. Above all, the nation-state has not only proved itself to be bellicose, but it has perfected weapons of war capable of ruining us all. The arguments for a new world order are indeed convincing.

He who has any familiarity with politics, national or international, knows that logic does not always determine the course of human events, and that, when it does eventually come into control, it makes its way slowly. The actions of men and nations are dominated by traditions, habits, indifference, lethargy, and fiery emotions. The mere fact that the nation-state with its conflicts has been the vehicle of progress for so many centuries gives it a momentum which will carry it on for many years to come, whatever its faults. For better or worse, the nation-state is deeply entrenched in the minds and hearts of mankind. We think in terms of sovereignty, national power, and nationalism, as our ancestors have done for centuries. Suddenly the scientist has made these concepts impracticable, even evil; but the experts in social science have not found the means of shifting human thinking to fit the new conditions.

The preamble of the UNESCO Constitution suggests the complexity of the causes of war in its statement, "Since wars begin in the minds of men, it is in the minds of men that the defences of peace must be constructed." The problem lies then not in the mechanics of international life, or even in the lack of mechanics, but rather in mankind. Often the statement is made that war is a natural product of present-day world society, and of course it is; but that society itself was constructed by men. Indeed we may say that in all man's known history he has never been able to set up a society free from war. This fact alone shows the immensity of the problem.

Can mankind construct a warless society? Although no categorical answer can be given to that question, it is appropriate to observe that psychologists believe that war is not essential to man's nature. Not the nature of man but the nature of his thinking is believed to be at fault. As someone has said, war is not "born into man, but built into him." Modern man is a nationalist, filled with conceit for his nation's accomplishments, and too easily inclined to hate alien groups. He wants his nation free to pursue its own good, untrammeled by consideration for the interests of others, and therefore he cherishes a concept of sovereignty which tolerates no restrictions upon the right to do as it pleases. He believes in the use of power to get what his nation wants if there is a fair chance that it will not backfire or be too costly. He does not understand the economics of international relations, nor does he care to so long as he and his countrymen are prosperous. He may even make so bold as to argue that it is the duty of the white man to govern underdeveloped peoples as colonies within an empire. Just how the minds of men can be cleansed of fallacious ideas and equipped with sound ones is the main problem of peace. Because the churches deal with men and with guiding men's thoughts, they are in a strategic position to be helpful here at the very point where world problems have their beginning.

The complexity of the task of contributing to the peace of the world, whether within the present structure of society or in a new order, is understood by some few churchmen at least. The leaders who drafted the Report of Section IV at the Evanston Assembly in 1954 properly asserted, "Christians must also face the fact that . . . peace will not be easily or quickly attained." Further wisdom was expressed in the statement, "Men's hearts must be changed." I might add that men's minds also need an overhauling. The churches are in a position to work on both the hearts and the minds of men.

V

A Democracy's Foreign Policy

The pivot upon which a discussion of church activity in foreign affairs must turn is the conception of democracy brought to the problem. What should a democratic people attempt to do in foreign policy? What should they leave to their government to work out alone in the conference rooms of the White House, the Department of State, and Congress? And at what points should they assume to dictate? Acceptable answers to these questions are hard to come by; yet they can make the difference between success and failure in our relationships abroad. Do the churches have any philosophy of democracy to guide them, as a moving force in American political thinking? Without one, no group can know when it is helping or when, perchance, it is meddling. What is the proper role of the public—the public of which the churches are a part—in foreign affairs?

More than a century ago the French writer Alexis de Tocqueville declared, "Foreign policies demand scarcely any of those qualities which are peculiar to a democracy; they require, on the contrary, a perfect use of almost all those in which it is deficient." He was thinking of the fact that public opinion in a democracy moves slowly, whereas diplomatic events rush along madly, indeed at a much faster clip today than ever before. Public opinion is subject to fits of irrationality, vacillation, or clumsiness—all fatal to the exacting business of maintaining stability and peace in world affairs. A mass of citizens, millions of them, cannot maneuver, as

48

can the President or Department of State, with patience, finesse, perseverance, attention to detail, and the secrecy required to foil an adversary. These inherent limitations of the people in foreign affairs must be given their due, especially when the adversary possesses the size and competence of Soviet Russia.

Although Walter Lippmann, in *The Public Philosophy*, and a number of other writers, have pointed up this profound problem of democracy's foreign policy, to date the American people have not grappled with it. The common assumption seems to be that the greater the number of popular directives drafted and placed before the eyes of government officials, the better. The logic behind it all —if anyone should care to bother himself with logic—would be that this is "democracy."

Ever since World War I, Americans have become more and more committed to a "democratic" foreign policy. Popular antipathy toward the Hohenzollern government of Germany which President Wilson did much to instill was readily broadened into a distrust of all governments in foreign affairs. This led to another one of those simple explanations of complex phenomena for which we so often search: war is the work of governments and their diplomats; peace can be assured only by popular diplomacy. The corollary to this alluring proposition seemed to be that the more the people substituted themselves for their government, the more peaceful and right our foreign policies would be.

This devil theory of government in foreign affairs has come to be the accepted thing in this country. An American entertainer invoked it when he said to American troops in a World War II battle area, "I wish that every diplomat in the world could spend a day or two at the fighting fronts—and this mess would soon be over." Americans like to quote Will Rogers' quip that "the United States has never lost a war and never won a peace." When in the spring of 1955 a "summit" conference was scheduled and President Eisenhower got ready to go to Geneva, the query went up in the press and on the air, "Will there be another Yalta?" Even a popular, conscientious, and Christian President could not be trusted when he left Washington to take on the role of a diplomat.

Open diplomacy is one of the inevitable demands of a distrustful "democracy" in foreign affairs. Diplomats are no longer allowed secrets, nor are they permitted to deal with one another in secret, because it is believed that they cannot be trusted to serve our interests. All transactions must be conducted in the public square. The result is that diplomats cannot bargain with each other to reach agreements, and negotiations quickly reach a standstill; we have what former Secretary-General Lie called "frozen diplomacy." Old-time diplomats like Hugh Gibson of the United States and Lord Vansittart of Great Britain have been particularly vocal in their denunciation of the new practice. They contend that by its nature diplomacy must be a matter of give-and-take, both parties receding from previous positions in order to come to an understanding which will end a dispute. This negotiators cannot do when diplomacy is open, for the people do not understand the need for diplomatic bargaining; they are willing to "take," but to "give" seems to them an unethical betrayal of principle. Working in the open, diplomats may discuss, argue, and even propagandize about the release of prisoners of war in Korea, German unification, East-West contacts, and the Middle Eastern problem, but rarely can they find solutions. "Bringing diplomacy out in the open" sounds like a purification process. But the glaring light of public scrutiny does more than purify; it dries up diplomacy. To be sure, the public can, as a rule, be given the *results* of negotiations without harm to the nation when the diplomats have finished their work; it is the process of negotiating which, in the interest of all, needs to be under cover.

The Bricker proposal to amend the treaty-making process is also based on a distrust of government, a belief that our officials cannot be safely permitted to make treaties for fear they will break down our democratic structure and deprive us of our rights. On the supposition that the men in the White House and in the Senate are or may sometimes be crooks or traitors, so the argument seems to run, we must cut down their power to act in our behalf. To prevent the government from doing something "bad," the Bricker people are trying to fence it in so that it will also be unable to do anything "good."

This same concept of democracy which holds government to be untrustworthy has led groups within the nation to swarm over their officials with advice. Whether these groups have studied the subjects or not, they relay to their congressmen or to the Department of State assorted opinions on technical assistance, loans to Spain, NATO, policy problems in the Middle East, and the Hungarian revolt. By this display of activity, they somehow feel that they are being good citizens, keeping the government walking the chalk line. They feel themselves thus to be expressing their loyalty to the "democratic" way.

To be healthy and sound, a democracy must be founded on popular confidence in the government. This is especially true in the representative style of democracy with which, for two good reasons, we in this country must be satisfied: (1) we have no assembly hall large enough to admit all 100,000,000 of our qualified voters in the direct-democracy style of the old New England town meeting; and (2) we have neither the time nor ability to deliberate wisely on the intricate issues of policy which crowd in upon the nation. Our chosen method is to elect men to take care of our foreign and domestic problems for us.

What is wrong with American democracy that we have so little faith in our government, particularly in the field of foreign affairs? Is it that we have lost confidence in our ability as a people to elect men of honor and rectitude to office? We have had very few scandals in officialdom to justify such an attitude, and nothing in recent years more startling than the discovery of an Alger Hiss in the Department of State. There have been mistakes of judgment in our policies, but how and where this side of Heaven can these be deleted from human conduct? Conceding for the sake of argument that our officialdom is somehow inferior, are not then these same distrustful people at fault? Is it not they who elected the officials now regarded as inept? If the answers to these questions be "yes," why do they not elect reliable men to office, rather than continue to choose men whom they do not trust and then hover over every official act with beneficent advice?

Where the people of a representative democracy will not place their confidence in their elected government, they are likely to succumb to either of two hazards. One, which might be designated the German way, is to turn to a powerful dictator who by oratory and promises wins popular support. The second, the American way, is for the people to crowd in upon the government, stifling it with advice, restrictions of power, undue publicity, and hostile criticism. As an old teacher of mine used to say, we Americans try "to cure the faults of democracy by more democracy." Or, in the words of Mr. Sisley Huddleston, we endeavor to run our foreign affairs by "crowd psychology."

At some points the record of the churches in relation to these abuses of democracy in foreign affairs is creditable; in others, it is not. The churches have criticized governmental policies in the democratic fashion, rarely imputing rascality or wholesale incompetence either to the government in general or to the Department of State in particular. They have never been conspicuous among proponents of open diplomacy; let us note, however, that neither have they advocated allowing diplomats to work secretly when openness might be damaging to American interests. The churches were not supporters of the Bricker proposal for tying the government's hands in treaty making; to the contrary, they registered opposition to the project, thus indicating a willingness to trust the President and Senate.

Where the churches have displayed a lack of confidence in our elected officials has been in their overloading the government with pronouncements and advice on concrete issues of policy. In order to influence the government, they confer with and send letters, telegrams and resolutions to the President, the Secretary of State, and the members of Congress; in legislative matters relating to policy, they delegate spokesmen to testify before congressional committees. To persuade the United Nations to adopt their policies, they dispatch through the C.C.I.A. of the World Council their representatives to U.N. meetings.

Although the churches seek in these many ways to influence governmental action, only one denomination, the Quakers, maintains a registered lobby in Washington. The National Council of Churches has an office there which serves as a center for contacts with the government, both in domestic and in foreign affairs, but

it does not have the status of a registered lobby. As earlier explained, the C.C.I.A. attempts by personal interviews and other
methods to influence governments everywhere into policies which
it approves.

Pressure on the government, whether by lobbying or by other
means, is the right and privilege of any group in a democracy. In
principle, our government is the voice of the people in matters of
policy, and therefore will hold itself responsive to public opinion.
If church leaders have a point of view on an issue, they are con-
stitutionally free to state it both to the public at large and to the
government. The question here raised is not on the legal or ethical
propriety of what the churches have been doing, but on whether
their activities along these lines have been or can be helpful to
the nation. Are they promoting or obstructing the efforts of public
officials? Related to this question is the broader one: Are other
private groups in the country which try to influence the government in foreign policy helping or hindering it?

Officials welcome the information and opinions which anyone
close to a subject can provide. For instance, when railway, agri-
cultural, and power interests some time ago apprised congressional
committees of their attitude toward the proposal to make the
Great Lakes and connecting waterways navigable for ocean-going
ships, the government obtained well-supported points of view from
leaders of thought on that subject. Or, when they listen to the
opinion of a missionary who has spent twenty-five years in India on
the subject of economic assistance to that country, they regard his
views as those of an expert. When a spokesman of the National
Council of Churches early in 1956 explained to the Senate Foreign
Relations Committee that a draft Treaty of Friendship, Commerce, and Navigation with Haiti did not include the provision
for religious freedom customarily inserted in such agreements, we
may be sure that the Committee was grateful for this reminder.
That the value of testimony and of opinions depends upon the
closeness to the subject of those giving them, is well understood
by anyone at all familiar with the ways of Washington.

Studies made by public opinion experts, men like Mr. Martin
Kriesberg, clearly show that administrators and members of Con-

gress are not equally impressed by all the opinions which come their way through letters, telegrams, and personal interviews. They are wise enough to know that a pronouncement by a Baptist convention will not be the opinion of all Baptists, that a statement by the National Council of Churches will not represent the thinking of all American Protestants, and that a position taken by the C.C.I.A. of the World Council will not have the considered support of world Protestantism. This by no means implies that public officials are indifferent to church opinion; it suggests rather that they take the opinions for what they are—those of a few leaders of better than average standing. Statements of opinion or attempted pressure on those rare subjects of policy which come close to church interests—diplomatic representation at the Vatican, freedom of religion abroad, or the chaplaincy in the armed forces—rather naturally carry more weight with public officials than those on the usual, run-of-the-mill type of issues.

When church leaders, or any group not closely related to a problem, set up their rather superficial opinions based on information gleaned from newspaper sources against those of the government, whose officials have the advantage of experience and access to facts and data which they alone can get, the functioning of our democracy is made to appear amateurish indeed. It suggests a revival of the doctrine of Andrew Jackson which played so vital a role in our nineteenth century spoils system, to the effect that any average man should be looked upon as capable of holding any office. Who can seriously propose that any average man should make foreign policy?

I shall not dwell further upon the complexities of foreign policy making; these were detailed in Chapter IV. What must be examined at this point is the capacity of the people to find their way about in the subject. A few years ago, Mr. Martin Kriesberg startled his readers (*Public Opinion and Foreign Policy*, edited by Lester Markel) by showing that 30 per cent of the electorate are "unaware" of any given event in foreign affairs, 45 per cent are aware but not informed, and only 25 per cent consistently show a fair knowledge of current developments. We may safely add that the information of the superior 25 per cent is based almost exclusively on news reports by radio, television, and press. In short, we Americans, with a few exceptions here and there, have neither the quantity nor the quality of information that would justify pressuring the government on the day-to-day issues of policy.

These "dark areas of ignorance" within the public should not upset us as they do, for they are natural and for the most part inevitable. We Americans are a busy people, our days so completely occupied by the wearisome job of earning a living that during our leisure hours we have little inclination to educate ourselves in foreign affairs beyond "getting the news." To examine books which would give us the history, economics, political science, geography, and other disciplines we need to analyze that news is and will remain beyond most of us; we do well to read occasional analyses in periodicals, or once in a while to scan a book with some relevance to international affairs.

Educational processes in or out of the schools, and efforts to prod the people may add to the capacity of the public to think on matters of foreign policy, as they have in the past. But, as long as men and women are limited in time and energy, their ability to make policy will remain meager in comparison with that of our officials in Washington. The subject of foreign affairs is so comprehensive that even officials of the Department of State who spend all their working hours on it are well informed, as a rule, only on their own respective areas of operation; one official will be qualified on African affairs, another on Latin-American, and a third on economic questions. When Mr. Elihu Root said over thirty years ago that, if the people insist on expressing their views "at all stages of diplomatic proceedings," they "must learn the business," he must have had his tongue in his cheek, for he of all people knew that the "business" is not easily or quickly learned.

In the light of these facts, what then is the proper role of the public, including the churches, in foreign affairs? First, let us concede that our views on policy, conveyed to officials by letters, interviews, and telegrams, can be of little assistance unless, having an unusually close relationship to the subject in question, we have a better than average opinion. Quality thinking rather than quantity thinking is the key to effective policies whether in a democracy or elsewhere. The churchwoman who has been led to believe that she is doing her Christian duty when she writes her congressman and urges him to vote more money for the Point Four program, although she knows little about the economics or social implications of technical assistance and nothing about the complexities of the United States budget, has been misled. Church leaders have been equally at fault.

Democracy need not be scuttled in order to allow this nation to play its part effectively in world affairs. The people have a role to fill in foreign policy, a vital role, even though it is not the one they have been trying at so clumsily. There can be no hesitation in affirming that, as the ones who suffer when diplomatic blunders eventuate in war and prosper when successes avert conflict, the people must be the "boss"—in this case a political boss giving life rather than death to democratic processes. This is in full harmony with that definition of democracy which holds it to be a political system in which the people "govern the government." This does not require, however, that they be present whenever a decision is taken, whenever diplomats negotiate around a table, or whenever the President dispatches a note to a foreign nation. The omnipresence of 100,000,000 or more adult Americans in government is not the key to democracy, but rather their presence—or at least the presence of those who are qualified to be vocal—at a few well-chosen, strategic spots. What are those spots?

Foremost among them is the election booth. Although the American people have long frequented this habitation of democracy, they are not always aware of the importance of the X-marks which they write after the names of their candidates within these small enclosures. Here it is that, as the boss of American politics, they hire their employees, the government, to work for them. Always, there are at least two groups of applicants, the Republicans and the Democrats, between whom the choice must be made. In the campaigns preceding elections the boss has an opportunity to get acquainted with these applicants and to find out something about the way each would try to advance his interests if given the job.

Because these employees—President, senators, and members of

the House of Representatives—will be hired for four, six, and two years, respectively, the boss cannot give them instructions when he selects them as to precisely what they will be expected to do. Issues may be discussed in an election campaign and the voter may get a line on the political philosophies of candidates, but specific mandates on foreign policy or on domestic policy can rarely, is ever, be given; with a dozen or two issues discussed in a campaign, it is obviously not possible to know the exact support from the people which each has won. Even if mandates were discernible, it would be unwise to impose them, for conditions change, and the people might not want their government to feel bound in 1959 by a mandate given in 1956. When, in the campaign of 1916, Woodrow Wilson was reelected President, he and his supporters made much of the fact that "he has kept us out of war"; yet as early as April, 1917, President Wilson faced conditions which both he and the people believed could be met only by a declaration of war against Germany.

All of this brings out another requirement which democracy places on the people as boss of their government. Having done their best to hire able men, their next duty is to give those men every opportunity to do a good job. The employee needs to know that his employer trusts him, both his integrity and his judgment. He needs to feel free to work behind closed doors, and to do things at times without consulting the boss. The people must be in contact with their government, to be sure, but they cannot hope for effective foreign policies if they remain at their employee's elbow nudging him constantly on this point or that. As stated before, some within the body politic, because of their closeness to a particular problem, may be in a position to advise and suggest, but most of us will create confusion rather than clarity by ill-considered admonitions.

In the employer-employee relationship, the boss will do most of his checking on things simply by being around and remaining alert. The government knows full well that its future career will depend on the satisfaction it gives; its controlling motive is always to please the people. The kind of foreign policies the people will get must depend, then, more than anything else, upon their own character—what they value most in life, and what their hopes and aspirations are—and upon being wide awake to see what is going on and to evaluate results. If the people are pleased with aggressive policies, these they will get; if they want cooperation in world affairs their government will emphasize United Nations methods and freer trade; and if they demand peace at any price they will likely be provided with appeasement policies. The kind of meals which the cook will set before his employer depends largely on that man's requirements—his likes, dislikes, moods, and digestive apparatus.

Here, by the way, is the clue to the opportunity of the church in foreign affairs, for in the long run the quality of a democracy is but the reflection of the quality of the people. As much as any institution in our society, the church gives the people character, shaping their philosophy of life, their ambitions and demands. It can do even more than it now does to "make" the boss of our democracy. I shall discuss this opportunity knocking on the door of the church in later chapters.

What if the government selected by the people and entrusted with the job of formulating just and effective foreign policies fails to measure up to the confidence reposed in it? This, of course, can happen and doubtless will occasionally. Here democracy comes forward with its strongest tool—the next election. If he be at all alert, the boss will know by the time the government's term of office comes to an end whether he is pleased with what has been accomplished. By the democratic process of election he can fire as well as hire. This is important not only because it enables him to get rid of an inept or a corrupt employee, but also because it is strong inducement for all employees to keep on their mettle in the task of serving the interests of the people.

To the question raised early in this chapter as to whether or not foreign policies can be democratically fashioned and controlled, my answer then is "yes" if, and only if, the people realize their inherent limitations and are willing to delegate authority to their elected officials. All Americans, including church groups, must make this their point of departure in their efforts to strengthen our foreign policies.

VI

Concrete Issues—Schism

The purposeful conviction of Christian leaders for some forty years now has been that the church "must find its way to the places where men really live," as Report II of the Amsterdam Assembly of 1948 stated. It must concern itself, so they think, with the concrete issues of domestic and foreign policy, making "the word of the gospel heard in the places where the decisions are made that affect the lives of men." The church needs, the Report declared, to recover "the spirit of prophecy to discern the signs of the times, to see the purpose of God working in the immense movements and revolutions of the present age, and again to speak to the nations with the authority of God."

Failure to speak out on concrete issues, in the opinion of most Christian leaders, leaves the church concerned only with general and rather lifeless principles of conduct. Delegates at the Evanston Assembly of the World Council of Churches in 1954 at times pointed out, in Dr. Walter Van Kirk's words, that "were the churches to do nothing more than to pontificate about moral absolutes at a time when the human race stood on the brink of total disaster, they would merit and almost certainly receive the condemnation of right-minded men everywhere." In their effort to relate Christianity to contemporary issues, they have taken stands on the League of Nations, disarmament, the Pact of Paris, neutrality, technical assistance, the Marshall Plan, loans to Spain, the Korean conflict, NATO, and scores of other questions, major and minor.

59

A term, "the responsible society," was coined at the Amsterdam meeting to describe the kind of social order that would be the objective of the churches as they grappled with political issues, domestic and foreign. The churches put themselves on record as seeking a society "where freedom is the freedom of men who acknowledge responsibility to justice and public order and where those who hold political authority or economic power are responsible for its exercise to God and to the people whose welfare is affected by it." At the Evanston Assembly, Report III made it clear that a "responsible society" is not "an alternative social or political system, but a criterion by which we judge all existing social orders, and at the same time a standard to guide us in the specific choices we have to make." Accordingly, the churches have set for themselves and for individual Christians certain standards— the dictates of God and the welfare of the people—by which to identify those policies which deserve their support. They believe then that they can translate the abstract principles of Christianity into the concrete programs of political conduct.

Ever since the churches began asserting themselves on concrete issues, a minority of their leaders have opposed the practice. In the resulting controversy, men like Dr. Karl Barth have argued that the job of the churches is to seek first the Kingdom of God and His righteousness, and that, if they do so, "all [that] we need in relation to the world's disorder may be added unto us." They believe that God is completely in command of our planet and its functioning and that He will see things through to a triumphant finish in His own way. Dr. Barth takes the view that "the care of the world is not our care. Burdened with this thought we could straighten nothing out." The root of human disorder, he believes to be this "dreadful, godless, ridiculous opinion that man is the Atlas who is destined to bear the dome of heaven on his shoulders." He opposes presenting the world with "Christian economics," or "Christian sociology." He is against entering into debate with the secularism of our age.

Prominent among proponents of the theological argument in favor of church efforts to solve the internal and international problems of the day has been Dr. Reinhold Niebuhr. He argues that the churches must be looked upon as instruments of God, busy in "the pulling down of the strongholds . . . [of whatever] exalteth itself against the knowledge of God." As a realist, he sees the fact of evil in the world and would employ the resources of the churches for its defeat. In his opinion, "It is certainly not right for Christians to leave it to the 'pagans' of our day to walk the tightrope of our age, which is strung over the abyss of war and tyranny. . . . It is particularly wrong if we suggest to these pagans that we have no immediate counsel in the present perplexity but that we will furnish a 'sign' of the 'coming Kingdom' by some heroic defiance of malignant power, if the situation becomes desperate enough." He believes in giving counsel that "this or that course may lead to tyranny" rather than "merely prepare ourselves to defy tyranny when it is full blown." The church, as he sees it, must cope with the anxieties, sins, and pretensions of human existence, not run away from them.

Most of us are not equipped to argue theologically about the proper role of the church in relation to political and world problems. To a layman the practical consequences of both the reasoning of Dr. Barth and that of Dr. Niebuhr seem fraught with danger. Either might serve as a foundation for an extreme position which, followed out in practice, could harm both international relations and the church. A more tenable position, pragmatically if not theologically, seems to lie somewhere between the extremities of thought advanced by these two theologians.

For the church to remain aloof from the pressing problems of the day and not to try to prevent or cure disorder would seem pitifully callous; not to use what capacity it has for the betterment of conditions of living would reduce it to a mere device for getting people to heaven. For this reason the Barth position is, as Dr. Niebuhr says, essentially eschatological. In joining the church a person would be concerned only with himself in eternity, not with his brother in immediate need; religion becomes committed to selfishness.

The other extreme, the ultimate logic of the Niebuhr position, could be equally vicious. The church cannot rush madly about from problem to problem, solving everything. Were it able to do so, then we should give it temporal power and let it make a reality of Utopia. Many problems, most of them highly technical, harass this world, and even experts, Christian experts, disagree about their solutions. No particular economic system, no social structure, and no project of world order could possibly be labeled "Christian"; the elements of a "Christian" foreign policy are equally debatable. Dr. Barth is right in saying that the churches cannot carry the weight of the world on their shoulders. But, admitting this to be true, should not the churches carry what little weight they can bear?

Why not recognize that the churches are by their very nature seriously limited in their capacity to deal with the problems of the world and then try to restrict their activities accordingly? Why not approach this question of the proper role of the churches in international affairs from a practical point of view and make its capacities and limitations the bases of its activities, rather than attempt to follow uncertain theological doctrine?

The limitations of the churches show up strikingly when they try to deal with the concrete issues of foreign policy. Perhaps none is more obvious than the fact that within the churches the elements of a Christian policy can rarely be agreed upon, whether by lay members or by the leaders. As Christians disagree on the meaning of Biblical passages, even within a single denomination, so they differ on the application of a given doctrine or ethical principle to a concrete problem. These differences of opinion preclude the possibility of a solid church front on most issues; and, when a position is dictated by a majority, the opposition of the minority renders that position unimpressive, even confusing.

The basic split in the thinking of Christian leaders which has handicapped them most in concrete issues of policy has been on the subject of war and the use of force in international affairs. The institution of war has always baffled the Christian church. The dominant attitude of the early Christians was strongly opposed to war. Men like Justin Martyr and Tatian in the second century, and Tertullian, Origen, and Hippolytus in the third, looked upon all war as organized sin; the canons of Hippolytus advocated excluding soldiers from the sacrament until they had done penance for their murders. When, in the fourth century, Christianity became the official religion of the Roman Empire, it was largely converted to the needs of the state; at this time Athanasius argued that "to destroy opponents in war is lawful and worthy of praise." In the fifth century St. Augustine tried to work out a logical system of thought: certain wars, notably those preceded by an injury, are to be regarded as "just," so he contended. A just war was, in his opinion, a procedure for the repression of wrong, having the quality of a punitive action or a civil suit. Since the time of St. Augustine this doctrine of just wars has been refined and modified by prominent churchmen such as Thomas Aquinas. The Augsburg Confession of 1530 expressly recognized the right of the Christian to wage "just wars," without going to the trouble of defining the term. Legalists, such as Hugo Grotius in the early seventeenth century and Emerich de Vattel of the eighteenth century, also gave the doctrine support.

Today Christian leaders in large numbers continue to espouse the concept of war as bad, even sinful, but nevertheless justified under certain conditions. Only a few years ago the Presbyterian Church in Scotland gave its backing to the idea, but without being able to agree upon anything definite as to the nature of a just cause. Such meetings as the Amsterdam Assembly (1948) of the World Council of Churches and the Evanston Assembly (1954) have given further evidence of wide support for just wars. What is even more important is the way in which many Christian leaders have rallied to the nation's cause as a just one when the United States has gone to war. Both in World War I and in World War II the majority of them quickly identified the cause of our nation with that of God and saw in the cause of the enemy only unmitigated evil. To be more specific, they have considered it to be their Christian duty to enter a conflict where they have seen the freedom, morality, and democracy of peoples to be at stake. Standing on the sidelines when a battle over right and wrong is on cannot be possible to a true Christian, as these leaders believe. Generally they would agree with a statement by Protestant Episcopal leaders in 1934 that "war is a mass movement for the attainment of an end which, upon a particular state of facts, may be good or bad. . . . No sweeping generalization is therefore possible respecting all war."

Alongside of this group who dislike war but find it to be justified on occasions, there is another, usually a minority, who can see no possible justification for mass murder and plunder. These people control some of the smaller groups, such as the Quakers and Jehovah's Witnesses, and they often make their presence known with great effectiveness within the larger Protestant denominations. The Kingdom of God to these people is a kingdom of non-violence. They cannot reconcile the Christian concept of God and man with the destruction and hate of war. For this reason, they would condone only revolutionary tactics of the Gandhi type. One of their number, Dr. Harry Emerson Fosdick, expressed their position in his statement, "We cannot reconcile Jesus Christ and war—that is the essence of the matter." He quotes the words of Jesus, "All they that take the sword shall perish with the sword."

This pacifist group has at times been large and vocal, more so in time of peace than in war. Even during World War II there were quite a number of conscientious objectors, not only from the peace churches like the Friends, but from the larger denominations—the Methodist Episcopal Church for instance. It was in the 1930's, however, that pacifism was strongest, appearing then often as the majority opinion of church leaders. In 1931 Mr. Kirby Page sent questionnaires to 53,041 clergymen on the subject of war and peace, and had replies from 19,372. Three years later he sent similar questionnaires to 100,490 ministers of the gospel, and received answers from 20,870. The following results were obtained in answer to the query "Do you believe that the churches of America should now go on record as refusing to sanction or support any future war?"

| | PERCENTAGE ANSWERING | | | |
| | 1931 | | 1934 | |
	Yes	No	Yes	No
TOTAL OF ALL RESPONDING	62	24	67	22
Methodist Episcopal	73	15	78	13
Presbyterian	53	33	57	30
Congregational	57	27	66	21
Protestant Episcopal	42	45	50	38
Baptist	53	29	62	26
Disciples of Christ	62	24	72	16
Lutheran	Not circularized		38	50

The following replies were received on a second question—"Are
you personally prepared to state that it is your present purpose
not to sanction any future war or participate as an armed com-
batant?"

	PERCENTAGE ANSWERING			
	1931		1934	
	Yes	No	Yes	No
TOTAL OF ALL RESPONDING	54	30	62	25
Methodist Episcopal	62	22	72	16
Presbyterian	46	39	51	34
Congregational	49	33	63	24
Protestant Episcopal	35	49	46	40
Baptist	46	35	57	30
Disciples of Christ	53	30	69	19
Lutheran	Not circularized		33	52

The significance of these figures could easily be exaggerated.
The questions were of such a character that they would, in all
probability, bring forth more answers from pacifists than from
nonpacifists, for the former are usually anxious to be heard whereas
the latter will not bestir themselves. The great majority of the
clergymen polled, it must be remembered, did not reply at all.
What the polls did show beyond any shadow of a doubt was that
in the early 1930's pacifism was strong within the ranks of Christian leadership, even more so in 1934 than in 1931.

Two efforts were made in the mid-1930's to find out what the
ordinary church member was thinking on the subject of war and
peace, one by the Northern Baptists and the other by the Congregational-Christian Church. Voting materials were sent only to those
Baptist churches which requested them, a total of 235; 9,601 ballots
were marked and returned. A little over 27 per cent of the voting
members thought they could best contribute to the cause of peace
"by refusing to bear arms in and by otherwise opposing any war
declared by my government." Approximately 42 per cent were
willing to bear arms and support the government "only in defense
of American territory against attack." About 25 per cent would
support a war if it were "a last resort after the government has
exhausted all peaceable means of settlement." These percentages do

not give a fair sample of thinking within the Baptist denomination at that time for the reason that voting was confined to those churches whose pastors requested ballots, and these would in all likelihood be the ones most pacifist in their views.

The Congregational-Christian survey reached about 200,000 persons, and therefore was much more representative than the Baptist. The results showed that only 6 per cent would support any war which the government might declare; 33 per cent would fight if our territory were invaded; 42 per cent would require that every means to peace be exhausted before going to war; and 15 per cent took the absolutist position of pacifism toward all war.

At the present time pacifist tendencies in the churches are less evident than in the 1930's. Like all Americans, the churchmen of today are disturbed by the menace to the nation's security posed by Soviet Russia's quest for world domination. The recurring crises and threats of the cold war make pacifism less alluring than in times of confidence. Whatever we may believe to be the injunction of the Bible on the use of force, somehow it is easier when confronted with danger to reach out for weapons of steel than to rely on the eternal verities. Few among us dare, like Gandhi, to face an enemy with ideas alone when he comes at us with arms.

Even today, however, the hard core of pacifism remains in the churches. This was apparent at the Amsterdam Assembly of 1948 in Section IV on "The Church and the International Disorder." After asserting that war is "a sin against God and a degradation of man," the Report of the Section went on to admit that in view of the total nature of modern conflict, "the tradition of a just war . . . is now challenged." The differences of opinion at Amsterdam were such that no unanimous answer was found possible to the question as to whether war can now be an "act of justice." In the light of these differences the Assembly could only say that there are three broad positions which Christians conscientiously take toward war, as follows: (1) supporting a war effort "may be a Christian's duty in particular circumstances," but it can no longer be "an act of justice" in view of the mass destruction which it produces; (2) supporting a war effort may still be regarded as a duty because, without a supranational agency, military coercion remains "the ultimate sanction of the rule of law"; or (3) refusing "military service of all kinds, convinced that an absolute witness against war and for peace is . . . the will of God."

At the Fourth Study Conference of the Churches on World Order at Cleveland in 1953 pacifism per se was not an issue, but the pacifist point of view came to the forefront on two occasions. When the security pacts of the United States—NATO, the Rio Treaty, and some of our Far Eastern alliances—were up for approval by the Conference, Mr. Harold Bosley of the First Methodist Episcopal Church in Evanston offered a motion against them. Later on, he also introduced a resolution against supporting United Nations action in Korea. Vigorous debate ensued in each case. In the votes which were taken, the Conference supported both the security treaties and the United Nations collective measures in Korea. The delegates who voted against approval—69 of the 215— were probably not all die-hard pacifists, but certainly most of them had pacifist leanings.

The Second Assembly of the World Council at Evanston in 1954 also acknowledged the disagreement of church leaders as to the proper attitude for Christians to take toward war. Section IV of the Assembly could agree only that "war is evil." Its Report went on to say that the churches "must study afresh the Christian approaches to peace, taking into account both Christian pacifism as a mode of witness and the conviction of Christians that in certain circumstances military action is justifiable." The issue of pacifism came up on several occasions, usually at the instance of some of the smaller peace churches whose delegates liked to remind the gathering of earlier ecumenical assertions that war is contrary to the mind of Christ; never, however, did it take on the dimensions of a major debate.

Centuries of disagreement among Christians as to the attitude which they should take toward war ought to convince everyone of the permanence of the cleavage. While it might seem less complicating if all Christians could agree not only on an attitude toward war but also on theological and other matters, the counterbalancing advantages of differing points of view must be recognized. These differences testify to the freedom of thought and conscience which is characteristic of both democracy and Christianity. A stereotype either in democracy or in religion would be unthinkable.

Whether the differences of opinion among Christian leaders toward war represent "diversity" or "division" depends upon how much the churches try to assert themselves on concrete international issues. The main reason why the Section on International Affairs at Amsterdam felt a "deep sense of perplexity in face of these conflicting opinions" was that it found action on contemporary issues hampered without a general agreement upon so fundamental a matter as war and peace. The churches must admit that here is a serious limitation upon their capacity to assert a Christian point of view on many international problems.

Mr. Arthur Darken tells us that at the Cleveland Study Conference one delegate said, "My Christian conscience will not let me vote to endorse military alliances like NATO." To this assertion another delegate retorted, "My Christian conscience will not let me do other than support the N.A.T. alliance, to help preserve justice and freedom as well as our own national security." These two delegates reflected only a "diversity" of opinion, a healthy and normal difference, until they were faced with a proposal that the Conference declare itself favorable to the American system of alliances; in the presence of an obligation to vote on a concrete issue, the difference of opinion became a "division." A divided church cannot speak with authority, either to the government which is responsible for foreign policies or to the general public.

The seriousness of the handicap which these differences of attitude toward war and force occasion in the treatment of concrete issues stems from the ubiquity of power in international relations. However much we may deplore it, the fact is that nations are engaged in an unending struggle to procure power which they can use to promote their interests and to enhance their security. Power is then a means to an end, so that a "foreign policy" which envisages an objective but lacks the wherewithal to reach it can be no policy at all. This, of course, does not imply that nations go around making threats of war daily in order to get what they want; but it does mean that always in the background of critical international controversies are the relative power positions of the nations involved. For instance, we have no difficulty in guessing how a diplomatic clash between powerful Soviet Russia and weak Finland would come out, assuming of course that other nations remain aloof from it.

The omnipresence of power in international affairs implies that almost every issue of foreign policy is one on which pacifists and nonpacifists are likely to split. The power issue has been unusually obvious in the United States policy of setting up and supporting NATO and the other alliances. It has been present, too, in the question as to whether our foreign aid program should be employed to build up the military strength of our friends and allies. It loomed large in the attitude taken by this country toward Iceland's demand in 1956 that we give up our bases on her territory. Questions of policy regarding the defense of Formosa, Russian threats in the Middle East (1956), and the uprisings in Hungary (1956) depended for answers primarily upon considerations of power. Divided as they are on anything as basic as power politics, how could the churches hope to pronounce Christian policies on these specific issues?

Where the implementation of a policy could be by nonmilitary means, the churches might be able to speak with the authority of greater unity. That national power can be economic, psychological, or moral, as well as military, we have come to learn in recent decades. The churches could agree to support the Marshall Plan, with its emphasis upon economic means in the reconstruction of Europe; the military implications of the Plan—the building of a Europe able to stand up against Russian aggression—were not so blatant as to arouse pacifist opposition. Agreement was general, too, on the Point Four program, whose connection with the military side of international affairs has been negligible. In basic policy issues where the nation's security is at stake, military considerations of one sort or another are, however, almost sure to stand out. Even in less important matters, the relative availability of military power lurks in the background of diplomacy—the bold fact that in a showdown one or the other of the negotiating nations could make its will prevail. It follows from all this that, when issues and situations in which military power plays a part are subtracted from the totality of policy problems, not much is left upon which the pacifist and nonpacifist elements of the churches might get together.

Many church stands on policy problems, like that taken by the Cleveland Study Conference on the alliances of the United States, reflect the handicap which disagreement on the proper role of power has created. In October, 1955, the National Council of Churches announced its approval of military action against the communist aggressors in Korea; in the vote on the issue five members opposed this endorsement as contrary to their consciences. In a somewhat different context, the divided counsel of the church was apparent, when in 1948, after three hundred clergymen had called on American youth to defy the new draft law, an article by the well-known clergyman, the Reverend Daniel Poling, appeared in the *Christian Century* sharply critical of those clergymen. Again, on July 26, 1950, the World Council of Churches at its third annual session commended the United Nations for its "prompt decision" to meet the aggression of the communists in Korea by "authorizing a police measure which every member nation should accept"; on the same day the pacifist Fellowship of Reconciliation issued a statement opposing the police action, asserting that intervention would "deprive the United Nations of the moral force which it might exercise if it resolutely refused to be drawn into the big power conflict." These clashing points of view on concrete issues within the area of power politics by church groups, all presuming to enunciate the Christian position, are perplexing to the onlooker. No wonder an editorial in the *Christian Century* on November 24, 1948, declared that "Church opinion on international affairs is confused. Christian leadership is hesitant and uncertain."

Where a proposed use of national power could be labeled "aggressive" rather than "defensive," the diverse elements within the churches might be expected to get together. For instance, it is a safe bet that pacifists and those who believe in just wars only would coalesce against any proponent of a "preventive" war on

Russia, by which we might beat the enemy to the trigger and destroy them first. Because no proposal to make a preventive war has been offered by anyone in authority, no official church statement on the subject has, of course, been formulated.

On occasions, a divided counsel on issues involving power has been averted by a burst of idealism, strong enough to submerge the differences which can divide churchmen. This was particularly noticeable in the 1920's and 1930's, when Americans generally appeared to be either indifferent to or ignorant of problems of national security and power. The churches, for instance, wanted disarmament and, like most Americans, thought little about the resulting power position of the free world and apparently cared less; they were guided only by the ideal of a warless world and the vision of its becoming a reality if Congress would spend less money for warships. Similarly, to keep this country out of war they, with other peace-minded Americans, supported the neutrality legislation of 1935–1939, quite oblivious of the probable effect upon the world of power politics.

Nowadays church leadership is more aware of the realities of power politics than it was before World War II. As Mr. Arthur Darken asserted in an article on "The National Council of Churches and our Foreign Policy" in *Religion in Life*, 1954–1955, many leaders have abandoned "perfectionist ethics." Soviet Russia has been teaching all of us the rudiments of power politics. Thus divergent attitudes within the church toward the use of force are now more divisive in foreign policy issues than they were in the 1920's and 1930's. Instead of being united by an exuberant idealism that overshadows differences, as before World War II, the churches now feel the handicap of the schism between those rejecting power politics and those willing to go along with it.

Whenever issues of policy are before the country in which the cause of idealism is identical with the cause of power, Christian leaders are again able to agree on a policy. For instance, dispatching wheat to hungry India appealed both to those who believe in charity and to those who want to improve the power position of this nation by keeping India outside the Iron Curtain. Again, the

Marshall Plan was at once an expression of generosity and a power device to hold Europe safe from communism. It is where the cause of charity and the cause of power are not so happily wedded that the churches can speak out only with the uncertain voice of a harassed majority.

VII

Concrete Issues—Problems

After a protracted discussion, the Southern Presbyterians, meeting in Harrisonburg, Virginia, in 1950, refused to make a pronouncement on the H-bomb, asserting, "We declined with the statement that we did not feel qualified to do so." Reporting the work of the session in the *Christian Century* of July 5, Mr. D. P. McGeachy said, "It ought to give us pause to remember that the great document on which our history as a separate denomination rests is openly and powerfully a defense of slavery. If we were wrong then we may be in need of correction now." Parenthetically it may be pointed out that the Southern Presbyterians were "wrong" for such a long time in their attitude toward the colored people that not until this Assembly of 1950 did they treat their Negro members without discrimination in living quarters and in the dining room.

This incident is cited here not in criticism of the Southern Presbyterians; on the contrary, they are to be commended not only for admitting and correcting their error, but also for learning from experience how easily mistakes on the concrete issues of policy can be made. What is most significant about the case is neither the denomination implicated nor even the final admission of the mistake, but rather its revelation of how "wrong" a church can be and remain for many years, even on a question essentially ethical.

To be sure, Christian leaders are not the only ones in the nation who have made mistakes in their advice on issues of foreign policy. Government officials themselves have been in error, although much less often than members of the opposition party in Washington would have us believe. To err is indeed human, and Christian leaders are no exception to the rule. All Americans who believed in 1928 that the Pact of Paris would prevent war were just as wrong as the church, and all those who assumed in 1941–1945 that we could adjust our policies to a long period of friendship and coopera- tion with Soviet Russia were equally far from the truth. It would be unfair to single out the churches for criticism from all the many groups of Americans who have held erroneous opinions.

This fallibility of Christian leaders in matters of policy would be nothing to worry about, were it not for the unique position held by the churches in our society. The layman easily equates the voice of the church with that of God. On occasions, indeed, religious spokesmen have gone so far as to claim for themselves a special prescience. A report of twenty-two theologians early in 1946 on "Atomic Warfare and Christian Faith," for instance, referred to the capacity of the church to "speak to men and women of any nation in the name of our Father and one universal community." Report III on "The Church and the Disorder of Society" at the Amsterdam Assembly in 1948 announced, "There are occasions on which the churches, through their councils or through such persons as they may commission to speak on their behalf, should declare directly what they see to be the will of God for the public de- cisions of the hour."

To the general public, errors on the part of those who seem to speak in the name of Christ are discrediting. People easily wonder whether the churches are as unreliable in religious matters as in secular. If the churches turned out to be wrong when they advo- cated American neutrality legislation in 1935 and thereby gave Hitler a green light for aggression in Europe, could they also be wrong when they tell us that we should love our enemies? If they spoke rashly when they said that the Pact of Paris would be a deterrent to war, did they also when they declared that the mis- sionary enterprise deserves our financial support?

The temptation of all who are authorities in one field is to lay down the law in alien fields where they have little or no competence. Mr. Robert Millikan was an eminent physicist whose opinions on scientific problems commanded respect, but when he lectured to a large audience of college students some years ago on politics his listeners rated him a "dud." With every good intention, too, Professor Einstein used to lower his stature as a scientist by extended advice on complex international subjects. The church has a large and respectful audience to which it can speak with authority on matters of religion and ethics. Can it address that audience on the specific issues of foreign policy without running the risk that its hearers will walk out on it when it gets back to the subject of religion?

A second problem inherent in pronouncements by the churches on concrete issues arises from the very nature of their speciality—religion and ethics. These are vital to the processes of policy making, and government officials who chart the course of our activities abroad will be at an advantage if they are anchored to firm principles of conduct. But when specialists in religion and ethics prescribe policy, their natural approach is to consider ethical principles only. They will ask and answer the question, "Does this proposed policy conform to Christian standards?" But there they stop. They rarely ask, and still more rarely answer, questions as to whether it is good economics, sound law, justified by the experience of history, or supportable by some kind of national power. To put the matter bluntly, they reduce all international issues to moral problems. They can do little else, for they do not have much of a hold on the economics, law, history, and politics needed, let alone the factual information and data possessed by the Department of State.

One result of this limitation of the churches is that their advice seems unrealistic. Another consequence is that the churches themselves are made to appear to the public at large as impractical. In short, they do not by their pronouncements on concrete issues help the government; and, what is worse, they harm themselves.

Another hazard of pronouncements by the churches on contemporary issues is that identification with one side in a controversy will very likely entail a corresponding alienation of the other. The alienated sectors of society, which may be thoroughly conscientious and perhaps even sound in their point of view, come to think of the churches as unfriendly, and avoid them. This loss of favor might be borne with equanimity if the churches would be sure that the stand they had taken was the only one possible to a Christian. But is this often the case? Is it not usually possible for a Christian to take any one of several attitudes toward a problem of foreign policy?

Take such an issue as American "isolationism" versus "interventionism" in 1939–1941. Was it not entirely reasonable and proper that a Christian should ally himself with either side? As an isolationist, he might argue that this nation could best advance the cause of right by keeping aloof from the war then raging in order to protect the homes of this nation from the rigors of a conflict whose outcome would almost certainly leave Nazi Germany or communist Russia dominant in Europe. As an interventionist, he could contend with equal propriety that this country should throw its strength on the side of the democratic nations, Great Britain and France, and defeat the selfish aggression of the Axis dictators. Why should the churches enter into a debate of this nature? When they support isolationism, the honest interventionist will be miffed; when they back intervention the isolationist is irritated by his spiritual advisers.

The consequences of taking sides appear to be understood by some leaders within the churches. This was evident at the Amsterdam Assembly (1948) in Report II, which admitted with some chagrin that the church traditionally has been too closely identified with the interests of the well-to-do class of society, and, as a result, is now in danger of being unable to win the workers. As the Report said: "The church in all countries has almost completely lost the working class. It speaks a language that they do not understand. Its interests seem to have no relation to their interests. Justly or unjustly, it bears the stigma of having been a staunch defender of the status quo, and of having identified itself with the cause of the possessing classes." How, with an admission of this kind, can the churches contemplate associating themselves with "isolationists," "interventionists," world federalists, or any other group which ardently promotes a cause in foreign affairs?

Rather similarly, the identification of the churches with the foreign policy of this nation, whether right or wrong, can alienate people in other nations whom Christian leaders are anxious to win, and among whom missionaries are working. Can Christianity have an appeal to the Asian peoples when it supports an American policy which they believe to be unsound, and perhaps even injurious to them, or when it denounces a cause which they cherish? Again the Amsterdam Assembly appeared aware of this danger, asserting in Report II, "In many parts of the world, the church is under deep suspicion of being an adjunct of Western imperialism and an agent of the foreign policy of states. It is widely believed that the messenger of the gospel is actuated not only by the pure motive of declaring good news but by political motives of which he may be himself half unconscious." When church groups declare themselves favorable to American policy in Formosa, for instance, as some have done, is it not natural for the peoples of India, Burma, and Indonesia, with their policy of neutrality in the East-West conflict, to think of Christianity as a phase of American nationalism, and therefore alien to them and to their interests?

The hazards, then, which the churches face by pronouncements on the concrete issues of foreign policy are those encountered by all political groups—the loss of influence when wrong, demoralization when defeated, and the enmity of others. To be sure, the churches of this country have no intention of playing the role of a political party. But like political parties they take stands on current issues and try to win supporters for their causes. Indeed, the ultimate logic of their present-day involvement in political issues would seem to be still more activity in politics. If they are doing their religious duty by championing one side or another of a political issue, why is it not equally their obligation to support this or that candidate for office? There are "good" and "bad" candidates for office, as there are "good" and "bad" sides to take on issues. Wisely, the churches desist from sponsoring candidates for office. Would they not be consistent to keep equally aloof from the issues of politics?

Whatever may be the connection, the power of the Roman Catholic Church in the minds and hearts of men and women of Western Europe has decreased as it has become more active in politics. Could it be that empty churches on Sunday are in part at least the consequence of their taking sides so much on issues that the individual has come to think of them more as instruments of politics than as means to salvation or goodness? True, the churches of this country are not likely, at least in the near future, to build political parties about themselves as the Catholics have in France, Italy, and Germany. But political involvements, great or small, on the part of religious bodies run much the same risks, with varying degrees of seriousness.

In a measure the approach of the World Council avoids some of these difficulties. Operating through the Commission of the Churches on International Affairs, it leans heavily on men with the background and time to study problems carefully. The C.C.I.A. might, perhaps, be wrong less often on the concrete issues of policy than the Christian leaders who formulate pronouncements within national conferences of denominational groups. The difference will at best, however, be one of degree, for anybody, "expert" or amateur, can be mistaken in the field of foreign affairs. Although Dr. Walter Van Kirk in the *Ecumenical Review* for October, 1954, made light of those who criticize the churches when "they speak about things of which they know little or nothing," the criticism stands.

The logic of this chapter is that the churches would be better able to carry forward their major work of redemption if they would desist from taking sides on the concrete issues of foreign policy. Does this line of reasoning apply with equal force to the individual minister of the gospel? Ought he in his sermons to criticize the government in matters of concrete policy or contend in behalf of this or that foreign policy? Should he relate his faith to the political issues of the day?

Certainly it is less serious for one minister to be wrong than for the entire church, as a national or state body. To be sure, as an "interventionist" he may alienate "isolationists" in his audience, or vice versa; most of us will readily remember instances of this nature in 1939–1941. Furthermore, when he advocates a certain policy, he may readily be identified with the political party or group sponsoring the same cause, and, on a hot issue, diminish the religious fervor of members of the opposition party in his church. These are risks which a clergyman will run when he tells his congregation what is right or wrong in any branch of politics, domestic or foreign.

My own humble opinion is that clergymen would do well to stick to their own job. If they cannot resist the temptation to talk in fields where they are amateurs, or if they feel impelled to refer to an international incident for illustrative purposes, my sensibilities are less aroused if they desist from advocating policies, and if they go to some pains to inform themselves rather more than is the usual practice. A few years ago, on the occasion of United Nations Sunday, I heard an excellent "sermon" in an Omaha church on the United Nations—not a plea for any particular attitude toward the organization but rather an exposition of its work and its many problems. The preacher did not say or even imply that, as Christians, we would err if we failed to support the U.N., if we preferred to promote world federation, or if we had an honest skepticism toward the idea of keeping the peace by any kind of international organization or machinery. I felt grateful to him for being willing to trust me, along with his other listeners, to reach our own separate views. He seemed interested primarily in informing or educating us. On my way home I thought over the purpose of his "sermon" and reasoned that an occasional, a very occasional, venture into the business of education on secular matters may be justified when a minister can do as well as this one. My fear was that not more than one in a couple of hundred preachers could do this well, and might better stick to the job of making men good rather than undertaking to make them wise. Then I wondered whether, if the churches really want their clergymen to hold forth on international subjects, they should not insist that their seminaries teach international relations to aspiring ministers.

VIII

Concrete Issues—Lead or Follow?

In *The American Approach to Foreign Policy*, the historian Mr. Dexter Perkins said, "The great Christian churches . . . have usually in the long run reflected the moods and the prepossessions of the societies in which they operate; they have not, in essence, determined these moods and prepossessions." Reflecting the views of the masses could hardly be the purpose of the churches in taking stands on concrete issues of foreign policy. They think of themselves rather as leaders marching somewhat ahead of the masses and of the government, lighting the way to peace and justice.

The special claim of the churches to leadership is the faith which they hold. They are not interested in foreign policy, as the labor unions and the Chamber of Commerce have at times been, to advance some material interest of dollars and cents. They want only a just and durable peace, and they believe that in the gospel they have the formula for its production. Their approach to foreign policy was expressed by the Evanston resolution on international affairs: "It is in obedience to Him, and through the eyes of our Christian faith that we look at the problems of this troubled world."

That the faith of the churches is a necessary ingredient of all good things we may take for granted. That it has a rightful place in foreign affairs will also be conceded. This one element of leadership in foreign policy making the churches have. But do they have the other elements—the skill, time, and knowledge? In the "faith

80

and works" combination to which churchmen often allude, no doubt about their possession of the former can be fairly raised; it is their "works," or more exactly their capacity for works, which dooms them to walk abreast of, rather than in front of, the rest of the crowd in foreign affairs.

In their thinking on foreign policy issues, church leaders are, indeed, little different from rank-and-file Americans; they are touched by the same influences and dominated by much the same fears, hopes, and interests. We are all loyal patriots; the flag adorns pulpits, dwellings, schools, streets, and business houses. We are all both rational and irrational in thought and action. We unite in a common desire for national prosperity and security. Behind all are the same traditions, history, culture, and democratic ideals. For our sons and daughters we cherish the opportunity for a good life, free from the hazards of atomic conflict. Living in similar communities, we go to the same kind of schools, read the same news in the same style of newspapers, and listen on television and radio to the same commentators. Whether as Americans we are the go-to-church type or the stay-at-home variety, we have about us this homogeneity of environment, and therefore bring to foreign affairs a similarity of outlook, interest, and ideology. Whether we are Christian leaders or agnostics, our opinions will reflect this common background.

Here is the reason why church-sponsored foreign policies are likely to be much the same as those of the general public. As Americans think, so is it natural for church people to think. If Americans are split on an issue, the churches will be similarly divided. No line separates the people from the churches or their spokesmen; the churches are a part of the great American society, as the people are a part of the churches.

Evidence is abundant that, where the churches or their leaders have taken positive stands on concrete issues of importance, their positions have almost invariably been reflections of the dominant opinion within the country. Mr. C. S. Ellsworth in a study of "The American Churches and the Mexican War," published in the *American Historical Review* (1940), explains that in 1846 church leaders in the Southwest, where expansionist sentiment was prevalent, approved the war with Mexico. He found similarly that the Congregationalist and Unitarian clergy of anti-Democratic and anti-Polk New England bitterly opposed the War. Churchmen, he believed, mirrored the opinions of the respective local communites of which they were part.

Enthusiasm in 1898 for a war to free the Cubans from Spanish oppression mounted within the clergy after the sinking of the *Maine*, as it did throughout the nation. The Reverend Thomas Dixon's admonition in a sermon against "hesitation, delay, diplomacy, and idle talk" struck a responsive chord in the emotions of many Americans; war was what the people wanted. President McKinley was reluctant to commit the nation to war, but he could not withstand the pressure which the public, including the churches, brought to bear.

After World War I, as we have already seen, the churches sided with that section of the American public which advocated membership in the League of Nations; although the United States remained aloof from the League it is probable that this position of the churches was in harmony with majority opinion within the country. From this point on, the stands of the churches on major issues have expressed the prevailing moods of the American people.

In the 1920's Americans, as earlier brought out, showed themselves to be novices at the tricky game of world politics into which they had been thrust by forces beyond their control. About the only thing which they felt sure about was that they wanted an enduring peace, a hope shared by all elements of society. Many who during the war had basked in the sunlight of idealism felt disillusioned by the selfishness of our allies at the Paris Peace Conference and by the failure of Utopia to materialize. They became the victims of their emotions and prejudices, unable to face international problems with resolution and to think their way through to rational policies advantageous to themselves and to the world. Some were confirmed dreamers, taking up with anything with the slightest suggestion of peace; they liked the ring of words and phrases like "disarmament," the "outlawry of war," and the "World Court," and they advocated such things blindly without examining their implications or the conditions essential for their success.

Others looked back to the days of American isolation from world affairs, the "good old days," and bent every effort to return to them and get rid forever of the evils of European power politics. Church people were to be found both among the dreamers and among the isolationists. Officially, however, the churches were almost always among the dreamers. They appeared to have no special talent, over and above that of other Americans, to be realistic. The bewilderment of Americans in general was also the bewilderment of the churches.

The 1930's brought some changes in American public thinking. In some quarters isolationism continued to thrive as debunkers told us that World War I had been fought in vain and that we would have been better off had we kept out of the embroilments of Europe. A Gallup poll in April, 1937, twenty years after America's entry into the war, disclosed that 64 per cent of the people queried considered our participation to have been a mistake. The jacket of *Road to War* by Mr. Walter Millis referred to "the frenzied years of 1914–17 when . . . a peace-loving democracy, muddled but excited, misinformed and whipped to frenzy, embarked upon its greatest foreign war. Read it and blush!" With so many Americans sharing this mood, it was not surprising that the neutrality legislation of 1935-1939 was enacted by Congress, denouncing rights for which our government had contended in 1914–1917, with a hope that the United States might keep out of the next war.

The 1930's also saw the beginning in this country of a better understanding of the facts of power politics. In part this may be explained by the open flaunting of power by Nazi Germany and fascist Italy, by their avowed programs of aggression, and by German theories of geopolitics and *Lebensraum*, widely read by Americans. Hitler's *Mein Kampf* and his speeches, circulating in their English translations, emphasized the same note of aggression. Aware that we were living in a jungle of power politics where sudden attack and death stalked on all sides, some Americans swung over to a "realistic" approach to American security problems. Men like Hamilton Fish Armstrong, Lewis Mumford, and Edward M. Meade reasoned that we could not by our wishing eradicate the jungle or separate ourselves from it: to exist we must be willing and able to fight. In short we must embrace power politics or become its victim.

The usual answer of the churches to the growing Nazi-fascist threat of the 1930's was neutrality for the United States. They were probably motivated less by isolationist dogma than by a determination to keep the country at peace, as the next best thing to keeping the world at peace; again, they went along with the dominant thought of the day. By this time, too, Christian leaders were inclined, like other Americans, to have little confidence in the League of Nations or in the Pact of Paris as means to peace.

As in the country at large, some headway for the cause of power politics was made in church circles before World War II. Reference has already been made to Dr. Reinhold Niebuhr and the small contingent of clergymen who became convinced of the inevitability of power politics and argued that this country must take part in them if the designs of fascist dictators were to be blocked and our security safeguarded. Throughout the 1930's Dr. Niebuhr wrote extensively on the subject, and in 1940, when the United States was debating the course it should pursue in the new war in Europe, he came out with his well-known work on *Christianity and Power Politics*, in which he argued that national power must be marshaled in support of the right.

When the general public in 1939–1941 went over to the program of helping Great Britain and France in what was believed to be a just cause, church leadership, too, became dominantly "interventionist." Minority voices to the contrary were audible, but, by and large, the opinions of Christian leaders during the two years prior to Pearl Harbor coincided with those of other Americans.

Apart from their pacifist sections, the churches have continued since World War II to take stands on concrete issues very much in line with majority thinking, and as a rule in support of the government's policies. All Americans were inclined, right after the surrender of Germany and Japan, to assume that our worries were over and to relax from strenuous international effort; the only appealing tasks immediately ahead were to bring the soldiers back home and to set up a United Nations. The churches fell in with these trends of thought.

Like other Americans, Christian leaders were slow to pick up the glove which Soviet Russia threw at our feet after the war. All of us winced at Russia's intervention in Iran in 1946, at her annexations of territory in eastern Europe and in the Far East, at her pressure upon Turkey over the Straits issue, and at her success in making satellites out of the small states of eastern and central Europe; but our dander was slow to rise. Our government was shocked, and it protested and argued, but not until 1947 did it settle upon a policy of "containment" to hold Russia in place.

The three postwar events which aroused the nation to the new danger also alarmed the church leaders—the communist pressure on Greece and Turkey (1947), the communist coup in Czechoslovakia (1948), and the invasion of South Korea (1950). When in March, 1947, President Truman asked Congress for funds to assist Greece and Turkey in their effort to combat the menace of communism, the Federal Council of Churches did not object to this new "Truman Doctrine," and appeared convinced that this display of American power in the back yard of Soviet Russia was necessary. No longer stressing forbearance by the United States and by Russia in their misunderstandings, as it had done in 1945–1947, the Federal Council in 1948 saw the danger that was shaping up and urged our government "to build conditions that would keep Russia from taking reckless and dangerous actions." The Council liked the Marshall Plan of economic assistance in Europe, proposed by the Secretary of State on June 5, 1947, and enacted into law in 1948. Usually the churches were inclined to favor economic and social programs over the military in the cold war now under way.

As stated earlier, majority church opinion came to the support of United Nations action in Korea in 1950. Later, when the nation became war-weary with the hostilities in Korea, so, too, did the churches, which urged measures of peaceful settlement, and in 1953 rejoiced with the rest of the country at the end of the fighting.

As the reckless idealism of a few decades back has been less prominent in American thinking of the last few years, so it has been less noticeable in church circles. Like other Americans, many churchmen talk nowadays about the "responsible use of power."

They rarely reach blindly for disarmament as in 1921–1922, but for a system of arms limitation "under effective international inspection and control," as at the Evanston Assembly of 1954. Indeed, so changed is American thinking today, both inside and outside the churches, from what it was in 1928 that it would be difficult to imagine ourselves getting excited over a new Pact of Paris renouncing war. In point of fact, the Russian government proposed in 1955 a multilateral nonaggression pact as an inducement to discard our present defense system in western Europe, but few were so naïve as to take it seriously. Today it seems to be assumed by the great majority of churchmen, as by most Americans, that this nation must play some part in international power politics.

Because of the close parallelism in church thinking and national thinking, an impatient editor of the *Christian Century* in the issue of November 24, 1948, took to task the Federal Council's pronouncements on world affairs. He accused the Federal Council of "too little independent thought and too complete identification of church views on foreign affairs with the bipartisan policy which prevailed in Washington." He went on to say, "So long as church pronouncements on relations with other countries consist of cautious and uninspired restatements of what church leaders believe is the mind of the state department, their pretension to offer creative leadership is a fiction." Of course, he was correct in asserting that Christian leaders have not shown signs of independent thinking and that they have had little to offer that has been new or different from the views of the country as a whole. But is this surprising? By what right can the church believe that, because it can lead the nation in its devotion to God, it is also fitted to lead in foreign policy?

To take up one specific aspect of the subject, there is every evidence that Christian leaders, both here and abroad, are quite as nationalistic as the rest of us, that they are no more detached in their outlook than other individuals who are their intellectual equals. In 1950, for instance, while the American churches subscribed to the American cause in Korea, the churches in Czechoslovakia, Catholic and Protestant, embraced the communist cause. Several of the Czech churches made public statements critical of

American "intervention" in Korea and denouncing the bacterio-
logical warfare of which we were accused by the Russians; these
churches even sent appeals to the Security Council of the United
Nations for hearings on the subject. Somewhat similar was their
dispatch to their brethren of West Germany in March, 1955, of
a message advocating opposition to the rearmament of Germany.
To be sure, these churches may actually have acted under pressure
from the communist dictators; we have no way of knowing the
extent to which they were the unwilling voice of communism.
It is hard to believe, however, that Czechoslovakian churches would
compromise themselves to the point of supporting a cause in which
they did not believe in order to be in the good graces of an unholy
government.

In West Germany, too, there have been signs that church leaders
easily fall in line with the nationalistic thinking of the country. In
1948 the United States occupation authorities reported that Dr.
Niemoeller and other churchmen, accepting the prevailing ideas
within the nation, had criticized the war-crimes trials and the allied
policy of denazifying the country. Like most other Germans, these
religious leaders looked upon the trials as acts of revenge. In
November, 1950, Dr. Niemoeller and thirty-seven other German
pastors sent a letter to Chancellor Adenauer in opposition to rearmament, another point of view widely held by the German
people.

This nationalistic bias in religious thinking was evident at the
Evanston Assembly in 1954. One churchman from an Iron Curtain
country protested against a report which, he said, had on it the
"trademarks" of Western ideology. He said, "I am here as a loyal
citizen of my country and as a Christian theologian who longs for
comradeship with his brethren."

In the discussions of the Report of Section IV on "The Church
and International Disorder" at the Amsterdam Assembly in 1948,
another Czech Christian displayed this same obedience to a strong
national loyalty. After a speech by Mr. John Foster Dulles attack-
ing the communist concept of society, Professor Joseph Hromádka
undertook an extended rebuttal. He contended that communism
represents, "under an atheistic form, much of the social impetus

of the living church." In his opinion Western fear of Russia had prevented a fair appraisal of what is really going on in communist nations. He warned in the spirit of a true nationalist that, if war between the East and the West should come, a victory for the latter would by no means be a sure thing.

Even in the matter of racial discrimination—a local rather than an international expression of nationalism—the churches in different parts of the world have been known to defend a prevailing local contempt for non-white peoples. The largest and most powerful Christian church in South Africa, the Dutch Reformed, has been adamant in its support of the government's policies of discrimination against native Indians and Africans, who, as we all know, constitute the great majority of the people. Other churches —Baptist, Congregational, Methodist, and Presbyterian—have adopted resolutions against the apartheid system. A few years ago Dr. Francis Hennemann, Catholic Bishop at Capetown, denounced the government's racial policy as "noxious, unChristian, and destructive." Separate churches for whites, however, remain common in the country.

The opposition of the leaders of some of the churches in South Africa to racial segregation must be looked upon as a healthy sign, evidence all too rare of the capacity of dedicated men to rise above the level of community thinking. The subject is one which is dominantly ethical in content and therefore eminently fitted for the attention of Christian leaders. That those leaders have not won over a larger number of church members means, however, that Christianity must still appear to the natives as a white man's religion.

Mr. Maurice Webb has recounted an interview which he once had with Mr. George Bernard Shaw on racial discrimination in South Africa. Mr. Shaw asked whether the natives were being taught Christianity, and received an affirmative answer. Then, related Mr. Webb, "He looked at me with his piercing blue eyes and said, 'Mark my word, young man, one day those natives will wake up to the fact that you white people are not Christian, and will declare a holy war upon you to turn you out of Africa in the name of Christ.' " Certainly Mr. Shaw was aware of the dynamite, as well as the democratic implications, of Christian ideas.

The Federal Council of Churches in this country on December 5, 1948, denounced racial discrimination, but it could scarcely be said that Christianity in the Southern states, where the problem is most acute, consistently follows this leadership. Many Christian leaders in the South have been fully aware of the incompatibility of the teachings of Christ with racism, but others, together with the majority of the laity, have appeared indifferent to the truth enunciated by the Evanston Assembly in 1954 that "the problems of race, difficult as they are, insoluble as they sometimes appear to be, provide for Christians an opportunity for obedience, and for a deeper understanding that bond and free, Jew and Gentile, Greek and barbarian, man of every land and continent, are all one in Christ." This lack of sensitivity to the implications of Christian doctrine was well illustrated by the memorial dispatched by 1,500 delegates of the Methodist Church, meeting at Charlotte, North Carolina, in 1955, to the Methodist Episcopal General Conference in favor of segregation within the church. Despite this local manifestation of racism, the Ninth World Methodist Conference of 1956 came out strongly against discrimination.

As churchmen, or rather the majority of them, are nationalistic where other Americans are nationalistic, so too are they like everyone else in their contempt for communism, their opposition to aggression, and even in their emotional explosions toward the Hitlers, Nassers, and Khrushchevs. Our weaknesses are their weaknesses, and our strength is theirs. With varying degrees of success, Christianity is at work among us all.

Leadership in foreign policy cannot lie with any special group within the body politic—whether that group be economic, educational, cultural, or religious. All have a part to play, a modest part; but all must remain in the rear, behind the government.

IX

Leaven in the Body Politic

Nothing fixes the quality of a nation's foreign policy more than the character of the body politic from whence it springs. "Our foreign policy," said a Department of State pamphlet in 1950, "reflects what we are and what we want." The ideology of a people—how they look upon religion, ethics, the individual person, and the state—must assert itself in the entire political life of a nation, whether domestic or foreign; it sets the goals of policy and marks out the avenues of approach to them. What the fundamental beliefs and assumptions of an individual are to his character and conduct, ideology is to the character and conduct of a nation. In Mr. J. P. Warburg's words, "What we must realize is that the public policy, foreign or domestic, in which a man believes, is the logical extension of the philosophy which governs his behavior as an individual toward the society in which he lives"; this observation is justification for the title which Mr. Warburg gave to his book *Foreign Policy Begins at Home.*

Mr. Feliks Gross, a student of foreign policy who recently wrote the book *Foreign Policy Analysis*, explains further this strategic relationship between ideology and policy. Foreign policy, he points out, is a "social process," and as such expresses the ideas which are at large within society. As he says, "There is a continuous interaction between the individual and society, and in consequence between the political ideas of an individual and the political ideas of a society." This relationship, he continues, makes it impossible

'to separate the political ideas of an individual from those of
ociety." The foreign policy of a nation, if these statements be
ound, can never rise above the quality of the people for whom it
peaks.

What institution within society is better fitted to shape the
haracter of a people than the church? To offer its constituency it
as the doctrines of its faith, unexcelled in their capacity to give
nen "the direction for their service, the obligation to share heartily
n the world's work and daily tasks, and the responsibility to seek
better social and political life," as stated by the Report of Section
II of the Evanston Assembly. This Report went on to affirm the
luty of the church to develop a "responsible society," a society
'where freedom is the freedom of men who acknowledge respon-
ibility to justice and public order and where those who hold
olitical authority or economic power are responsible for its exercise
o God and to the people whose welfare is affected by it."

The gist of this reasoning is that by making people sensitive to
he demands of Christianity, the churches incidentally make their
nost vital contribution to American foreign policy. If this were not
rue, Christianity would indeed be a lifeless thing, alien to the
laces where men live. Alive in the mind of a man, it will affect
is conduct everywhere, whether in business, school, sports, na-
ional politics, or international relations. When the churches con-
end that it is their duty to "relate Christianity" to the concrete
ssues of foreign policy, they err; rather it is for them to build men
nd women who—within the body politic, each for himself—will
elate their religion to life in their own way.

By the nature of things the churches cannot do a perfect job
f inculcating Christian virtues into the minds of those who, as
ublic officials or members of the public, run the government. A
ealization of this fact is one reason why clergymen feel the urge to
ackle the specific issues of foreign policy themselves. Unwilling
o rely upon those whom they have taught to play the proper role
f a Christian, and unmindful of their own shortcomings, church
eaders issue pronouncements setting forth desirable and undesir-
ble policies for the nation.

For the most part, the churches have done well in adding the leaven of Christianity to the body politic, even better perhaps than they realize. In this country no leader is completely unaware of Christian tenets, and none would be so brash as to denounce them publicly. No political leader would admit indifference to them in his conduct, however much in fact he may ignore them when no one is looking. Many leaders—Presidents and secretaries of state included—have been exceptionally loyal church members; President Eisenhower and Secretary of State Dulles are both deeply religious men. President Wilson's religion shone through all his philosophy of foreign policy, and if he had matched his Christianity with a better understanding of power politics he might have been even more successful than he was. All through our government are men whose religion has added to their usefulness as public servants, men like Dr. Ralph Bunche, a distinguished product of the Greater King Solomon Baptist Church of Detroit. These men can be trusted to relate their religion to their work without specific instructions from the churches as to what the policies of their office should be.

When he seized control in Germany, Herr Hitler encountered and largely eradicated this leaven of Christianity before he was able to go ahead with his diabolical policies at home and abroad. Before coming to power he had said in *Mein Kampf* and in the famous "Twenty-five Point Program" of 1920 that he stood for religious freedom, but once in office he found Christianity to be an obstacle. To neutralize the leaven he taught the German people doctrines of hate and expansion—the Aryan myth and the pseudo-science of geopolitics; many people accepted them but others did not. To weaken the leaven at its source he went to work to curb the churches.

The Nazis tried to capture Protestantism from within by means of the German Christian Party; failure in this enterprise left the church split. Opposed as he was to any religious influence in political affairs, Hitler then set about to unify the thirty rival subdivisions which had existed within the church and bring them all under the authority of the state, with Dr. Jager as Commissioner of the Evangelical Church. In 1936 that Church issued a Manifesto learly revealing its plight with a statement that "the question is whether the Christian faith is to retain its right to exist."

The Catholic Church in Germany also came to be looked upon as an obstacle to be reduced before the Nazis would be able to realize their objectives. Even before he came into power, Hitler had fought with the Center Party, which had at its core a strong Catholic element. As Chancellor in 1933 he concluded a Concordat with the Papacy, hoping thereby to eliminate future misunderstandings. But the Catholics opposed his program at several points, particularly his law of sterilization and his educational policy of removing the German young people from the Church schools and monopolizing their training.

With the heavy hand of dictatorship the Nazi state left no stone unturned in its zeal to convert the churches from obstructive to cooperative elements within its all-important body politic. As Reich Minister Hanns Kerrl said, "The Nationalist Socialist State cannot suffer any 'state-free spaces' which might serve to disintegrate the nation." The churches were compelled to goose-step along with the army.

To say that Christian virtues can be helpful to a nation in its foreign affairs does not imply that they alone can do the trick of solving its problems or of saving it and the world from ruin. Goodness and decency have their place in foreign policy to be sure, but so do many other human or national attributes—intelligence, knowledge, persistence, caution, resourcefulness, and even power. Mr. Sumner Welles brought this out in his statement that "innumerable foreign policies, like the road to hell, have been paved with good intentions." A nation which could see foreign policies only from the angle of good intentions might, like the same kind of individual, be a blundersome idiot. What is more, it would be well on its way to the graveyard. Christian precepts are one, but only one of the qualifications of well-equipped policy makers.

To get down to brass tacks, what help can Christianity offer in foreign affairs? What is this leaven of which we have been speaking? Presumably, the answers to such queries will be found within the realm of ethics and idealism, for it is here that the Christian faith operates. A few illustrations will be in point.

To begin with, a Christian nation will be considerate and reasonable in the objectives toward which its policies will be directed Like all nations, it will be guided by motives of self-interest, and will therefore seek for itself a reasonable security, but in doing so it will also respect the security interests of others. An "enlightened self-interest," as President Eisenhower refers to it, could never be used as a cover for the annihilation of a neighbor for security purposes, as Nazi Germany annihilated Austria, then Czechoslovakia and Poland in 1938-1939, or as Soviet Russia crushed Estonia, Latvia, and Lithuania in 1940. An enlightened self-interest will recognize that strengthening the economies and the security of others will also strengthen oneself. It will also see in a stable world order, whether achieved by a United Nations or some other organization, an advantage to itself.

A Christian nation will also be selective in the means which it employs to advance a defined objective. Its government will know, even without being told by the churches, that there are some things that it cannot do without provoking hostile criticism at home. Falsehood, deceit, trickery, and guile will not be tolerated by a Christian people. Acts of aggression or threats of aggression will be tabooed. Respect for the rights of other states, large or small, will be demanded. A willingness to employ peaceful methods of settling disputes with other nations will be manifested. As earlier asserted, Christians will, however, not always agree on what procedure is ethical, especially in their attitude toward the use of force and participation in power politics.

A Christian nation will understand that in foreign policy, as in all human conduct, there is realism in a healthy idealism Standards of decency in conduct win friends among the nations and produce an atmosphere of confidence, whereas unethical conduct makes enemies and engenders suspicion. Good will generated abroad for itself will be an element of strength or power to a nation. This is a rule of conduct not understood by the Nazis of Germany, who pushed other countries about so shamefully that when the World War broke out in 1939 their potential enemies covered the map, not only in Europe but throughout the world Russia under Stalin was also indifferent to the rule of decency in its expansionist policies, in breaking its pledged word, propagandizing with lies, robbing small nations of their independence, and converting neighbors into satellites. After Stalin's death, the new Soviet leaders appeared to be aware of the practical utility of friendliness, and went abroad dispensing economic assistance, kind words, and smiles. That these methods paid off, we found out to our dismay, as the new atmosphere of confidence loosened the bonds of our alliances and turned the attention of the neutral world toward "peaceful coexistence." Then, in 1956, when the Soviet Union sent troops into Hungary and threatened to intervene with force in the Middle East, these advantages she had won quickly vanished. Once again the world realized that communism has no scruples as to the means of attaining a desired end.

That the churches have impregnated the American body politic with ethical concepts which have helped to keep our foreign policy decent must be conceded. Although Secretary of State John Hay and Secretary Dulles stretched the point when they said that our policies are founded upon the Golden Rule, nevertheless strong moral foundations have underlain our conduct. We have not always been circumspect, especially in the Western Hemisphere, where moral lapses have been embarrassingly obvious: our conquest of Mexican territory a little over a century ago; our canal diplomacy in Central America in the early years of this century; and our frequent interventions before 1933 in the internal affairs of the Latin-American nations. Despite these delinquencies, the penchant of Americans has been and remains respectful of the proprieties; our economic policies, more than our ethical conduct account for Vice President Nixon's misadventures of 1958. During the past twenty-five years, even our Latin-American record has been creditable. After a recent trip to Latin-America, Mr. Robert Frost reported that the people there like us for our "decency." Mr. Frost approved of this decency, saying that while it "gets us into a lot of trouble, it pays in the long run."

In his book on *The American Approach to Foreign Policy,* Dexter Perkins discussed at some length the moral qualities of Americans in foreign affairs. He brought out the traditional American distaste for imperialism and the reluctance with which we took colonies from Spain in 1898. He described how we were troubled by a bad conscience after President Theodore Roosevelt maneuvered to get canal rights from Panama following the Panamanian revolt from Colombia in 1903, and how to assuage it we arranged in 1914 to pay Colombia $25,000,000 in "conscience money." Similarly, we agreed to pay Mexico in the Treaty of Guadalupe Hidalgo (1848) $20,000,000 for the California territory we had taken, and after the Spanish-American War we gave Spain the same amount for the Philippines. After the Boxer affair with China in 1900, our conscience would not allow us to take any indemnification from that country and we remitted the money she had agreed to pay us, on condition that it be used for the education of Chinese students in America.

Some there are who believe that we Americans are too ethically minded in our conduct toward others. An excess of decency where decency is called for would be hard to imagine. This is not the mistake we have made.

Where Americans often err is in seeing nothing but ethics in the issues of foreign policy. Even where no substantial ethical factor exists, as in the question of the recognition of communist China, we will insist on concentrating our attention on the "good" and "bad" in a situation. Red China should not be recognized, so the argument runs, because it is bad, guilty of aggression in Korea and of intervention in the Indo-China fight; the Reds kill off their political opponents, and they infiltrate their neighbors. All this is, by our standards, "bad." But it is largely irrelevant to the question of recognition. In fact we now recognize Soviet Russia, which is fully as "bad" as Red China. Why not, in any case, take into account our interests—that by recognition we shall (1) be able to negotiate with Peiping on our common problems, (2) be better informed as to what is going on in China, and (3) be in a stronger position to use our influence to split the communist world? How can a nation convert its enemies into friends if it will not talk with them?

This inability which many of us have to see anything but ethics in a foreign policy issue is probably a holdover from our long isolation from Europe and from power politics. The British-dominated Atlantic Ocean was security to us in the nineteenth century; should the ocean have dried up, the British policy of preventing an upset in the European balance of power was there to protect us. Safe and secure, we did not have to think in terms of power, as the nations of Europe were obliged to do; when Americans thought at all about foreign affairs, which was infrequently, it was largely to moralize. Suddenly, with the advent of air power and nuclear weapons, the ocean has shrunk to a narrow creek, while at the same time British might has largely spent itself and no longer shields us. Obliged to seek security for ourselves in our own foreign policies, first from Germany and now from Russia, we have learned the hard way that ethical principles alone do not protect us from an enemy. But as Americans have become more realistic, they have not given up their old habit of seeing ethical issues at every turn. Our arguments still center on "this is good," or "that is bad," whether we are talking about the recognition of Red China, the NATO Alliance, economic aid to Tito, or the Baghdad Pact.

One danger which we face in this connection is that, while learning to think about foreign affairs in terms of hard facts and national interests, we may cease to apply ethical principles where they are genuinely at stake. An approach to foreign affairs which fails to give both to ethical principles and to realities their proper due could be fatal. Although Americans still cling avidly to the ethical approach, too much so, those who know the American temperament fear that from too much we may someday swing over to too little, especially if the Russian menace continues. What more constructive purpose could the churches, the keepers of the nation's conscience, serve than to help us hold on to ethical principles when they properly apply and always to encourage respect for hard facts?

This unending day-to-day job of trying to make and to maintain a body politic fitted by its ideology, particularly in its ethical outlook, to be a conditioning element of American policy offers no quick road to peace. Patience and fortitude are demanded for its performance. Where patience is lacking, the temptation is to employ what seems to be a quicker method—direct advice on the concrete issues of policy. But the indirect method in the long run will prove to be not only quicker but more sure.

Those of us who, as teachers, have struggled with the problem of making good citizens out of young Americans have learned the greater effectiveness of the indirect approach over the direct. Only the context in which church and school work differentiate them, after all, for both deal with the minds of men, trying to turn them into paths of righteousness; each in his own area educates our society. We who educate in the schools have a natural urge to spell it all out in detail and tell the youngsters in front of us that to be good citizens they must support the things that we ourselves believe to be sound. Many of us would have them subscribe to the reciprocal trade program, although a few teachers might argue against it. Some of us would advocate the United Nations idea, but others would criticize the U.N. and point up the advantages of world federation. There are teachers who think that a good citizen should support NATO, whereas others are skeptical. Whatever our views, they seem to us so right that we are strongly tempted to indoctrinate impressionable minds.

Not much experience in teaching was needed to teach me that I could not make a student into a good citizen by telling him what to think. For one thing, I can never feel too sure of the answer myself in an issue of specific policy; the opinion which I hold about the worth of the United Nations may turn out to be wrong. Furthermore, many students do not want to be told what they must believe; give them a dogmatic "truth" on a subject of policy, and if they are smart they become suspicious of you. Even were I sure of the truth and able to sell my ideas to my students, I have succeeded in making them good citizens only on a few pending issues; I have not taught them how to find the truth a few years hence when some other issues come to the forefront, and I am not around.

The better way to make a student into a good citizen is to tell him, not *what* to think, but *how* to think about the problems of national and international life. We can show him that to think about any problem of politics, he must have some factual information, and we can help him learn how to get it. We can acquaint im with theories—economic, social, or political—and help him to analyze and assess them. We can give him a sense of honesty in thinking and help him to divest himself of prejudice and bias. Even when we have successfully taught a student all these things and he knows how to think effectively in political matters, he still will not be a good citizen unless other institutions within society have done their job. From the church and the home he must learn about religion and morality, thus becoming sensitive to issues of right and wrong, and to his duty as a responsible person within a responsible society.

So it is with the churches in the field of foreign policy. They will accomplish little by trying to tell the people and the government what specific policies are sound and what are unsound; the truth is far too illusory, and those who dogmatically claim to know it open themselves to suspicion. The better course for the churches to pursue is to help, along with the teachers and the family, to build better men and women who together will constitute a society of quality, a society fitted by its ideology and character to play its proper role in foreign affairs. As the teachers may help to train people how to think, the churches may continue to inculcate an ethical outlook which will give our policies a proper ethical content. If, together, the schools, churches and homes produce a superior body politic, then superior foreign (and domestic) policies will follow as surely as the day the night.

X

Education in International Affairs

Ethics and idealism in foreign affairs the American body politic has in abundance, thanks to the Christian teachings of the churches. To be well rounded, it needs now to develop a better understanding of world affairs. We must match our idealism with a healthy realism founded on a knowledge of cause and effect in the relations of nations.

The churches have for several decades been active in educational work within the field of international affairs. I shall not plead with them to busy themselves more than they do now with such activities. Indeed, I shall not plead with them at all. My sole purpose in this chapter is to suggest ways in which their educational work could be made more effective without engaging any more time and attention than they now devote to the subject. I have no magic to offer, but after many years of experience in the teaching of international affairs, I make bold to claim a knowledge of what people need to learn.

The objective of education in international affairs is not a nation of experts; that would be neither possible nor desirable. My contention all along has been that foreign policy making is not the business of the people but rather of the government, whose officials have the time and the information necessary to the task, as well as an army of experts at its right hand for consultation purposes. The role of the people (apart from special interest groups) is to set limits on what the government may do, not by rushing into

Washington with a carload of quick and ill-considered advice on every concrete policy issue, but simply by acquiring and holding a few sound opinions on the fundamentals of international relations. If the people, that is to say those people who take any interest in world affairs, are soundly educated in a few basic principles of international trade, government trade policies will not go far wrong. If the people know a few elemental facts about power politics, the government will be aware of what it can do with alliances or with the United Nations without receiving a deluge of hastily written letters from all over the country when a specific issue is before the nation. When the people are right on the fundamentals, government policy will be right; when they are wrong, government policy is likely to be wrong also. The people can be right on the fundamentals with much less effort and skill than would be required to know what they are talking about on the many changing issues of policy.

Back in 1922, when a popular interest in foreign affairs was just beginning to assert itself, former Secretary of State Elihu Root said: "When foreign affairs were ruled by autocracies or oligarchies the danger of war was in sinister purpose. When foreign affairs are ruled by democracies the danger of war will be in mistaken beliefs." One major war and a half-dozen minor ones fought since that statement was made, plus the untoward course of recent world events, suggest that popular participation in foreign affairs has been founded on some of the "mistaken beliefs" to which Mr. Root alluded. Most international trouble, to be sure, can be traced back to the dictators of Germany and Russia, whose policies have been dominated by "sinister purpose." But this country must shoulder some of the blame, for we have been guilty of beliefs which we can now recognize as completely "mistaken." Our ignorance of the basic facts and forces of international relations has been so great that we (1) have thought it possible to get enormous international debts paid over a high tariff wall, (2) have counted upon communist Russia becoming a peaceful neighbor after the power of Germany on the one side of her and of Japan on the other had been smashed, and (3) have given away billions for foreign aid without deciding what, if anything, we might reasonably expect in the way of a return.

To state it bluntly, thinking on foreign affairs in this country has tended toward the superficial, both inside and outside the churches. Like all highly complex subjects, foreign affairs lend themselves to casual, armchair speculation, on the general theory that "my guess is as good as anybody's, and nobody can prove with equations that I'm wrong anyway." Because they realize that the present state of world affairs is one productive of war and therefore in need of reform, our finest people are tempted to get into this guessing game of international politics. Mr. Charles Marshall was right, if unnecessarily caustic, in his remark that "foreign policy appeals to those inspired by identification with large and high-sounding causes. Its complexities and subtleties are rich with opportunity for generalizers and obfuscators."

Quality rather than quantity is, of course, the key to an effective public in foreign affairs. To double the size of a thinking public which thinks badly is hardly constructive; it would indeed be destructive, for it would require the government to move even more uncertainly than now, as it awaits the slower formulation of the opinions of a larger public. For this reason the churches or any other group bent upon strengthening the democratic foundations of American foreign policies should be satisfied with a small audience, measuring success by what they do to enlighten a few rather than a large number of their listeners.

Emphasis upon quality in the educational process automatically rules out indoctrination. Those of us who have observed the indoctrination programs of dictatorships, the Nazis of Germany and the communists of Russia, are well convinced of their dangers; not a thinking people but robots are produced by such programs. The principle deserves repetition that in a democracy education must be dedicated to providing men and women with the tools for reaching their own conclusions, not with ready-made "truths." As Boyd Bode said in *Democracy as a Way of Life:* "Democratic education is obliged to stake everything on a program for the liberation of intelligence. It need not and must not demand uniformity of belief. . . . It is not to such uniformity of conclusion but to certain habits of thinking and feeling and acting that democracy must look as its hope for the future."

As between the basic forces or principles of international politics and current information, it is the former which have been most shunned, even by the educated. Yet how can a person have a sound opinion on the American policy of economic assistance abroad without understanding a few principles relating to international trade, and how can he think straight on technical assistance without knowing something about problems of industrialization? How can he have an opinion on the peace work of the United Nations or on the merits of an alliance such at NATO without familiarity with the principles of power politics?

A person who is unwilling to equip himself with a few basic principles, as well as a modicum of information, on a problem of policy ought not to presume to express an opinion. There is no disgrace in silence, for nobody can speak convincingly on everything, and he who is not competent to pass judgment on one subject may be effective on another. Public opinion is at its best when it is the opinion of the qualified, few in numbers though they be. The general public can, at most, be vocal only on those occasional issues of importance which come up once or twice in a lifetime, as in 1898 on the question of war with Spain; it is the "sleeping giant" of politics, rarely aroused but terrible in its might.

Soon after World War I, as the American people were developing a new interest in foreign affairs, the churches became convinced of the need for an educated public. They were determined "to create the will to peace," as the *Discipline* of the Methodist Episcopal Church stated its objective in 1924; they were out to "launch an aggressive campaign to teach the nature, causes, and consequences of war." The Methodist Church in 1928 set up a Commission on World Peace and provided it with $15,000 a year for its operations. After four years of work this Commission reported that its program of education was "reaching every member of the church and church school," chiefly by means of its periodicals and instructive materials. In 1930 the Methodists sent seven of their young men to Haverford College for a two-week training course in international affairs; thus prepared, these young men took part in fifty-eight institutes attended by about 31,000 young people throughout the nation. The following year the American Friends Service Committee trained thirty-four Methodist ministers to carry on a similar educational campaign at Epworth Institutes. Pamphlets on such subjects as *Disarmament, Patriotism,* and *Jesus and His Principles of World Peace* were widely circulated.

Most of the major Protestant denominations, particularly in the northern part of the country, went in for educational activities of this nature. The Presbyterian Church in 1936 established a Department of Social Education and Action to educate not only for peace but for other causes within the field of social relationships; even earlier, through its Board of Christian Education, the denomination had been active. Study materials for courses lasting as long as three months were widely distributed with lessons on such topics as "How We Can Help to Bring About World Peace," "The Christian View of War," "The Causes of War," and "How War Can Be Abolished." Sunday-school publications were full of articles and stories designed to promote friendly international relationships. The young people's paper, *Forward,* during 1929 and the first five months of 1930 carried twenty-two articles on peace and world friendship. Topics of war and peace were taken up at summer camps and in denominational colleges. The Department of Social Education and Action encouraged the establishment of committees in the various synods and presbyteries to carry forward the educational efforts of the church; by 1938 there were twenty-two synods and 158 presbyteries equipped with these agencies.

In addition to the educational efforts of the separate denominations, there were many of a cooperative or interdenominational venture. The Fellowship for a Christian Social Order tried to elevate Christian thinking on international subjects through its magazine *The World Tomorrow.* Religious groups were prominent in the work of the National Council for the Prevention of War, whose resources were devoted to world organization, disarmament, and world-wide education for peace. Through its Commission on International Justice and Goodwill, the Federal Council of Churches in America labored diligently to advance world understanding. Perhaps most outstanding of all its educational activities was the arrangement of "study conferences," some of which, even before World War II, attracted wide attention in the country; during the war those conferences worked with skill on the problem of setting up a just and durable peace when the fighting should come to an end. The quality of the pamphlets distributed by the Federal Council for that purpose was distinctly superior.

Ever since the 1920's local churches have called in to their meetings outside "experts" to address them on international topics. These speakers have included public officials, professors from nearby colleges and universities, travelers, and persons close to the League of Nations, the United Nations, or perhaps UNESCO. Occasionally these addresses have been a part of an extended group study of a special subject, such as disarmament or technical assistance to underdeveloped peoples.

Without abatement the educational activities of the churches have continued since World War II. Local "workshops" like the one held under the auspices of the Connecticut State Council of Churches in October, 1953, at Middletown, have been set up from time to time. Pamphlet material and articles in church periodicals on world affairs are still published, although less voluminously than before World War II. A year or two ago, the annual conference of the Church of the Brethren meeting in Colorado Springs adopted a resolution that it seeks "to deepen the convictions of their young people of the futility of war." Late in 1954 a Virginia Institute on the Chuches and World Order met to study means of reducing tensions between Soviet Russia and the free world.

The National Council of Churches, successor to the old Federal Council, remains active in educational work. Among its activities nothing has been so conspicuous as its arrangement of several National Study Conferences. Meeting over a period of several days, one of these conferences listens to able speakers, and in its various "sections" discusses contemporary problems. The National Study Conference on World Order held in Cleveland in 1953 recommended, among other things, that the churches set up their own study groups to examine the problem of revising the Charter of the United Nations, a subject which in 1955 was to be on the agenda of the General Assembly of the U.N.

The Commission of the Churches on International Affairs, operating under the World Council of Churches, is also dedicated to the cause of education. This phase of the work of the Commission, Mr. Werner Kägi has recently pointed out, is "only in its initial state." He explains that there is a realization that "church members and the general public must be kept properly informed about important international issues and made to realize their responsibility in relation to them."

All of these educational efforts of the churches are in many ways admirably conceived, and certainly they are inspired by a genuinely Christian concern for the future of mankind. As in all educational efforts, the good accomplished cannot be measured in the precise terminology which we apply to things—pounds, inches, or cost. No one can say positively how much, if at all, they have improved the quality of American thinking. But those of us who, in one capacity or another, have had contacts with church discussion groups and with religious publications, are convinced that there are conspicuous defects in the programs of the churches. We would disagree sharply with the statement that "the churches traditionally have sought to dive below the surface of human disorder to get at basic causes." Occasionally there is a will to go beneath the surface, but more often the surface has not been penetrated.

The gravest error of the churches, like that of other groups of citizens which arrange for discussions of international affairs, is in concentrating on subjects of contemporary interest at the expense of basic principles. When the Israeli-Arab dispute has been in the headlines, they have called in speakers to enlighten them on that problem. Late in 1955 when the United Nations was approaching its tenth birthday, discussion groups throughout the country liked to schedule meetings on the U.N., perhaps on "The First Ten Years of the U.N." Speeches and round tables on the recognition of Red China, the Formosa problem, Russian penetration into the Middle East, and the revolt in Hungary have all been popular at the time when those issues were in the news. Discussions of such topics are in no sense undesirable. The criticism is not that items of contemporary interest are taken up, but rather that they are the only ones given any considerable attention.

Why not go into the fundamentals of international relations more often? Subject matter which will help a person understand day-to-day events rather than the day-to-day events themselves is what is most needed. Many recent world problems stem from the challenge of nationalism in Asia and Africa to the old imperialism. It takes the form of demands by the people of Algeria for independence from France, of revolt by the Greeks in Cyprus against British domination, or of rebellion in Kenya against the British. Why not study nationalism or imperialism, or both, and thus obtain tools for the analysis of such problems? In view of the fact that Soviet Russia is nowadays behind many of the issues of policy faced by governments everywhere, why not study the theory of communism and its adaptation in Russia, or the nature of the foreign policy interests of the USSR? The principles of international trade or those of international investments are always a "must" for an understanding of the economic phases of world politics. Because of its importance in international affairs, the United Nations deserves to be studied intensively—its origin, structure, activities, and problems. The nature of power politics is always an item on which Americans need a better education. Most of these subjects would require a series of sessions by a round table. They are also topics which could be treated in church pamphlets and periodicals. Unless church people are willing to face up to tough assignments of this character, they will never crack the surface of American inaptitude in foreign affairs. Admittedly, basic subject matter is less spectacular than the controversial issues of the day; but the current disputes which we deplore, despite their fascination, develop from the lack of proper attention to the fundamental.

That the quality of public thinking, rather than the quantity, will show up in the substance of foreign policies is clear from a study of public opinion made by Mr. P. K. Hastings and published in the *Political Science Quarterly* (1954). He brought out that opinions of the informed and the uninformed will agree when little in the way of information or understanding of principles is called for, or when a "stereotype"—the Monroe Doctrine, national sovereignty or some such concept—is involved. But where information or a knowledge of principles is required for straight thinking on a problem of policy and no stereotype is present, the opinion of the enlightened few differs markedly from that of the ignorant.

In her recent volume on *Common Sense and World Affairs*, Miss Dorothy Fosdick of the Department of State asserted, "Never, I suspect has so much energy been put forth by so many people to get a nation educated in foreign policy." The country has been flooded with speeches, pamphlets, articles, and books intended to educate us in foreign affairs. That they have benefited us so little may be explained by their emphasis upon reaching the many with superficial information on contemporary problems rather than upon invigorating the thinking of the interested few by educating them on the basic material of international affairs—nationalism, imperialism, principles of trade, sovereignty, ideology, power politics, and problems of world organization.

XI

Wisdom in the Body Politic

In an introduction to Mr. Louis Halle's *Civilization and Foreign Policy*, former Secretary of State Acheson said, "We Americans in our study and writing on international relations have tended to shun theory and logical historical analysis of historical material." We have, to put it bluntly, failed to devise for ourselves basic attitudes, convictions, and perspectives. We have no philosophy of international relations to anchor our thinking. The net result is that current problems place demands upon our intellectual and moral resources which we cannot meet. We therefore face the issues of foreign policy unsteadily, erratically, and emotionally, like the adolescent who has not yet found himself.

A valuable by-product of church educational work on the basic facts and principles—nationalism, imperialism, power politics, communist ideology, economic theories, and so on—would be the boost it would give us toward the development of a philosophy. Indeed, if the churches are to take any kind of interest whatever in world affairs, they, too, need to grapple with topics of this nature and at least become familiar with defensible positions on the fundamentals.

Were it possible for a church group—local, national, or international—to reach conclusions on any of the fundamental forces which lie beneath the concrete issues of the day, public statements of its findings could not be objectionable. To be sure, strong differences within the churches, such as between pacifists and nonpacifists, might prevent agreements widely enough supported to deserve publicity. It goes without saying that publicity to findings could never be constructive in the development of a public philosophy of foreign affairs unless those findings were based on adequate study and deliberation; off-the-cuff opinions from any group are meaningless.

"Pronouncements" on the fundamentals of international relations, widely supported and thoroughly prepared, offer advantages which the pronouncements of today on the concrete issues of policy could never embody. The former would be directed to the body politic where they would stimulate public thinking in foreign affairs; unlike the latter, they would not be dispatched to government officials for adoption as policies. Furthermore, pronouncements on the fundamentals can be formulated by a study of source material readily available to the general public—books, publications of the Department of State, periodicals, and newspapers; they do not require the classified and restricted information, now available only to governmental officials, which is essential in dealing with specific issues.

The Evanston Report on International Affairs stated and elucidated a number of pronouncements on the fundamentals of international relations; how well they were understood at Evanston or how widely held is not clear, but it is apparent that the serious thinking of at least a few people went into their formulation. The Report noted several "minimum conditions" to coexistence with communist nations, bringing out points which most people needed to consider. Then, under the heading "What Nations Owe to One Another," the Report stated the following general principles: (1) the members of the world community are interdependent; (2) nationalism is an "obstacle to international cooperation" when it exists as an end in itself; (3) imperialism, the "exploitation of one people by another, in any form, is evil and unjustifiable"; (4) the United Nations principle of trusteeship should be extended; (5) the self-determination of peoples should be recognized as a legitimate right, and nations with dependencies should "take reasonable risks in speeding progress toward this goal"; and (6) technical assistance to underdeveloped peoples is "one of the brightest pages of recent history."

At the end of these pronouncements on some of the basic principles of international life, the authors of the Report came back to the familiar church point of view—that it must also take positions on the concrete issues of the day. In asserting that because international conflicts "do not yield to broad generalizations" the churches would authorize their Commission of the Churches on International Affairs to speak for them on specific issues, they erred grievously. It is only to "broad generalizations" that conflicts will yield. To what else other than fancy or whim could they yield? And what except "broad generalizations" can the public or the policy maker use in thinking about the concrete? If the churches are to write off "broad generalizations," on what conceivable ground can they claim for themselves any role at all in foreign affairs, for what have they to offer except the "broad generalizations" of Christianity? Is it not because the broad generalizations of Christianity are presumed to be useful in prescribing the details of human conduct at all levels, whether individual or national, that churches go to some pains to teach the principles of Christian ethics to their members?

If it be true, as stated earlier, that a sound American philosophy of international relations will incorporate some well-considered generalizations on nationalism, how are we to get them? Are the churches interested in working on the subject? The statement of the Evanston Report that nationalism is an "obstacle to international cooperation" when it exists as an "end in itself" is far from adequate. It assumes that nationalism can exist for some purpose other than to serve itself. Is this possible? Many other questions must be tackled if we are to have a working philosophy on nationalism. Well-considered opinions on such issues as the following would be welcome:

Is nationalism an element of national power which cannot be given up as long as self-defense is necessary to a people?

Can nationalism be kept from its excesses, or like all emotions will it at times be uncontrollable?

Is nationalism a cause of war?

Is nationalism Christian?

What are the causes of nationalism?

The Indian philosopher Tagore believed nationalism to be "adolescent." Is it in fact a characteristic of an immature people or even an immature world?

Imperialism, too, needs further elucidation. Evidences of church opposition to it have been plentiful in recent years as the great empires have been challenged by the nationalistic peoples of Asia and Africa. But as yet the churches have given us little or nothing in the way of reasoned generalizations on questions like the following:

Is imperialism consistent with Christianity?

Can imperialism be a benefit to subject peoples?

What are the motives behind imperialism?

What problems follow the decay or destruction of an empire?

Should a dependency have its freedom when it has shown no evidence of capacity for self-government?

Should a right of self-determination be recognized?

Could the trusteeship system be improved or extended? If so, how?

To help Americans formulate sound generalizations on such matters would be a more effective way to promote sound foreign policies than to come out with a pronouncement asking the United States Government to support the Algerian natives against France. When the Federal Government deals with a concrete issue of this nature, it must consider not only the principles of imperialism held by it and by the people, but other matters which few members of the general public are equipped to handle: (1) the effect American support to the natives would have on French participation in NATO; (2) the security and welfare of more than a million Frenchmen in Algeria, were France to get out; and (3) the effect which American support to France would have on our relations with the Arab and Asian countries.

Again, the churches might study the subject of technical assistance, and then come out with a pronouncement for or against it as a principle; to do so would be much wiser than to adopt a pronouncement on some specific issue relating to the subject, as for example, asking Congress for a larger appropriation for the purpose without any examination whatever of the problems involved. Or they might investigate the idea of coexistence with communist nations and announce their findings, instead of advocating something specific like the renewal of negotiations with Soviet Russia or abolishing the H-bomb. They could examine the general idea of foreign aid and tell us their conclusions, rather than adopt a resolution to be sent to Congress against aid to Spain or to Yugoslavia.

Nothing more basic could be done to help this country in foreign affairs than to give us some sound thinking on the question as to whether policies should reflect primarily the nation's own interests or an unselfish desire to improve the world and the lot of its people. This conflict—self-interest versus idealism—projects itself into all conduct, whether of nations or of individuals. In ancient Greece, Pericles recognized the alternatives and maintained that Athens followed her ideals. President Wilson has been criticized on the ground that his philosophy of foreign policy was too idealistic, concerned only with his League of Nations when it should have given more heed to the security needs of this country and its allies. Nowadays many thoughtful men and women incline toward a balance of self-interest and idealism, and against the excesses of either. Whatever view a person or a nation takes on this fundamental matter is bound to reflect itself in the substance of policy; it will, for instance, bear directly on the subject of foreign aid: whether any aid shall be given, or whether a program of aid shall be adjusted to the promotion of American security needs or to the improvement of living standards abroad. On occasions, to be sure, a policy will at one and the same time advance the national interest and serve the welfare of others; the intervention of the United States in Korea in 1950 was justified both as a security measure and as a humanitarian project for saving a weak people from enslavement by their communist neighbors. Considerations of this nature, involving motivation in conduct as they do, fall definitely within the churches' sphere.

The risk which Christian leaders would run in handling a basic problem of this character is that they might impulsively jump over to the side of idealism without adequate study and discussion of the realistic factors involved. By the nature of their calling, clergymen are bound to be men of high idealism. Are they prepared to relate their ideals to the hard facts of world politics? Are they open-minded to the truth that policies devoted principally to the making of a better world could be disastrously enervating were a nation to combat even a small percentage of the evil abroad in the world? Is it right to occupy ourselves so exclusively with the eradication of evil elsewhere as to weaken our capacity to protect ourselves and to give a reasonable prosperity to our people? Is Mr. Richard Osgood right in saying that we must make realism the "balance wheel of American foreign policy"? President Eisenhower and Secretary of State Dulles favor the idea of "enlightened self-interest," as they call it; the opinion of Christian leaders on the merits and implications of this formula would have ready listeners.

The suggestion that the churches should deal with the general rather than with the concrete, and thus contribute to an American philosophy of foreign policy, does not imply that all of us would be fitted into a stereotype of thought. Out of such a process certain attitudes might come to prevail throughout the nation on imperialism, idealism, power politics, or coexistence, but there would always be dissenters. Only in one respect would there be any hope of making those people who concern themselves with foreign policy alike: that they can think constructively out of a background of principles—not necessarily the same ones, but for each person those of his own conviction.

No expectation is held either that the churches would fit themselves into stereotypes in the generalizations reached on the fundamentals of world affairs. If a consensus on some subjects were to appear, it would be significant in the development of a Christian philosophy of international relations. Where differences persist, as they no doubt would on subjects relating to pacifism and power politics, the challenges of each to the philosophy of the other should be stimulating; a division of opinion in an enterprise of this nature would not make the churches appear ridiculous, as it does in the pronouncements made today with an air of finality on the concrete issues of policy.

The distinction between the fundamentals of international relations and the concrete issues of policy is usually clear and obvious. In July, 1956, it seemed somewhat blurred, however, by the action of the Dutch Reformed Church in relation to western New Guinea. That territory, the last remaining vestige of Dutch imperialism in the East Indies, has been claimed with persistence by the new state of Indonesia ever since its successful revolt against the Netherlands; like other possessors of colonies, the Netherlands tries to hold on to its dependencies, and therefore has rejected the Indonesian claim. The Dutch Reformed Synod considered its duty in relation to the matter, and decided that it "must bear witness to the responsibility it owes to God and to our neighbors." It decided wisely that "it is not the duty of the church to put forward a solution to this problem." Then it proceeded to call attention to considerations which it believed should be in the minds of those responsible for a solution. It said that "everywhere in Asia and Africa things are changing. No longer does the community of nations regard the relations between certain European countries and the Asian and African regions as the sole concern of those European countries." Further, it suggested that "there is every reason to ask ourselves if our motives are really free from selfishness." It also raised the question as to whether "the Christian freedom of the inhabitants of New Guinea who are won to faith in Christ is really served by the close ties which they think exist between the missionaries and foreign rule." These statements were put forward as general principles to be applied in deciding on the future of the territory, but they were obviously slanted toward a definite policy—turning the disputed land over to Indonesia. They raised a storm of protest within the Dutch public, on the ground that this kind of action is not a proper function of the churches. The incident shows, among other things, that if the Dutch churches had earlier studied the subject of imperialism and formulated some generalizations on it, they would have felt no need in 1956 to take a stand on what amounted to a specific issue.

Perhaps the greatest benefit to be gained from work by the churches on the fundamentals of international relations would show up in the broad area of war and peace. The point was made in Chapter IV that the institution of war goes back ultimately to the ideas which men hold, to the philosophy or lack of philosophy which people everywhere bring to bear on world problems. President Roosevelt pointed out in the 1930's how incongruous it was that, with almost all of the people of the world so set against war, we were nevertheless plunging headlong toward World War II. In the 1950's, again, people have been demanding peace although there has been warfare in Korea, Indo-China, North Africa, Hungary, and the Middle East; and we have lived in constant dread of World War III.

Why are the nations so helpless in this vital matter of war and peace, constantly producing the wars which they seek to avoid? Is not the answer to be found in the fact that the fundamentals of popular thinking, the philosophies with which international problems are approached, do not harmonize with the lofty objectives of the people? They have little or no understanding of cause and effect in foreign affairs. They are trying to run a powerful machine without knowing how to give it direction. Were they to manage their business affairs with as little understanding as they employ in their international relationships, they could not long stay out of bankruptcy.

Internationally the nations are in fact in bankruptcy, and it is largely because so few even among their most thoughtful people understand the great principles and forces that have been mentioned in this chapter—nationalism, imperialism, power politics, sovereignty, communism, and conditions of trade. We assume blithely that we can retain the hatreds, conceits, and selfishness which are the usual concomitants of nationalism and at the same time enjoy a harmonious world order. The Arabs hate the Jews and vice versa; patriots in the United States form "America First" organizations; and the Germans pursue their national aspirations completely indifferent to the national aspirations of the French. The French insist on holding on to the advantages of an empire, in complete defiance of the principles of nationalism at work among the peoples of North Africa and Indo-China.

Today communism is the main enemy of democracy, and one of the strongest forces for disorder and war now at large, yet few among us could state its basic tenets. How, then, can we think coherently about such questions as coexistence, Russian disarmament proposals, and the new look which appeared in Russian diplomacy after Stalin's death?

Within the imperialistic nations are people who assume that they can hold tight to their colonies or satellites while at the same time the reign of peace will continue indefinitely. Would the Russians build up an empire in eastern Europe, or the French persist in holding on to their empire, if they understood the interaction of cause and effect in nationalism and in imperialism? Can Americans strive for an enduring peace in a world of imperialistic machinations without this same knowledge of cause and effect?

Are the churches equipped to go into the fundamentals of international relations and thus to aid in building a more perceptive American outlook toward the problems of today? One thing is crystal clear: if they are unable to perform this function, they are in a still weaker position to undertake the more complicated and delicate job of telling the government what to do in the concrete issues of policy. If they are not equipped to master the economics of technical assistance, they can scarcely claim to be capable of giving advice on the precise amount of money Congress should appropriate for the purpose

In so far as organizational matters are concerned, the churches are fully as well equipped to deal with the fundamentals of international relations as with day-to-day policy problems. On a worldwide basis they have the World Council and the C.C.I.A.; nationally there is the National Council of Churches and the assemblies and committees of the separate denominations; and on a state and local basis the denominational and interdenominational bodies which now deal with contemporary international issues are available. Another asset in the way of equipment is the superior quality, intellectually and morally, of church leaders. If there is anything the churches lack, it is the stamina to tackle international relations from so difficult and challenging an angle.

Working on the fundamentals is less appealing than issuing pronouncements on contemporary problems. It involves solid, hard work much like that done by college students on class assignments or by a diligent Sunday-school class. It is less exciting than the purely contemporary phases of world politics. It belongs to that category of labor whose results can rarely be seen in any tangible form, and never measured.

If church leaders are unwilling to give the time and effort needed for a job of this nature, it is difficult to see how they can justify remaining in the stern, demanding field of international relations. No amount of advice on concrete issues of policy, which the churches are rarely able to give constructively, can make up for a task undone in the fundamentals—a task which they are admirably fitted to do.

XII

International Ethics

In its Report on International Affairs, the Evanston Assembly of 1954 said that "underlying the more obvious barriers to a genuine world community is the lack of a common foundation of moral principles." In a later passage the Report added, "The world of nations desperately needs an international ethos to provide a sound groundwork for the development of international law and institutions." Indeed, it is true that nations do not have a common code of moral principles to guide them in their conduct toward one another, and this lack is a handicap to orderly relationships. High officials of the United Nations have often called attention to the cross-purposes of the member states which result from differing ethical standards; objectives and methods acceptable to one state will be vehemently denounced by another.

To be sure, there are reasons for the present-day low estate of ethics in international relations. In the mid-1920's, Professor John Dewey wrote an article in *Foreign Affairs* in which he pointed out the untoward consequences of the disfavor, at least outside the Catholic Church, into which the doctrine of the law of nature fell during the nineteenth century. For centuries it had furnished criteria both for individual and for state conduct, providing among other things an essential tool used by Hugo Grotius in his *Law of War and Peace* (1625), a book which served as the foundation stone for modern international law.

The law of nature was understood to consist in those rules of conduct deemed to be valid universally at all times and places; by many it was equated with the law of God. Courts consulted it in the decision of cases, as in 1822 a United States Circuit Court in *La Jeune Eugénie* ruled that the slave trade was contrary to international law chiefly because it was "repugnant to the great principles of Christian duty, the dictates of natural religion, the obligations of good faith and morality, and the eternal maxims of social justice." During the nineteenth century the law of nature was gradually replaced by the concept of positive law, so that the actual practice of nations rather than ethical principles came to be emphasized. What nations do in fact, rather than what they should do, is now the basis of international law.

As long as it was consulted, the law of nature gave to Christendom a principle of ethics and a method of law widely recognized. This does not imply that it purified international relations, for in fact nations were quite as hard-boiled in their attitudes toward one another as they are today. It did, however, offer criteria of action to which appeal could be made, and a principle which, had it not been discarded, might have served as the medium for the further incorporation of ethics and law into standards of national conduct. With no recourse to the law of nature, the Christian world found itself without the theoretical foundation it needed to inject ethical principles into the doings of the nations.

Professor Hans Morgenthau in his *Politics Among Nations* offers as another explanation for the present lack of standards of conduct in international relations the shift away from absolute monarchy which began several centuries ago and accelerated rapidly after the French Revolution. When Christendom was ruled by a clique of kings and emperors who knew one another personally and often were related either by blood or by marriage, it was natural to think of international relations as governed by the same code of conduct as that obtaining in personal affairs; within this kind of society of nations a national delinquency was at the same time a personal affront. True, in those days sovereigns were quite as inclined to lie, steal, and trick their adversaries as are governments now, but at least there was a standard, an accepted standard, by which such acts could be condemned once they were identified. As in every ethical system, of course, controversy and quibble might arise as to whether certain alleged misdemeanors had in fact been committed, and rationalization was always a possible resort of the evildoer.

Today few monarchs remain, and few of those have any substantial constitutional authority, so that international relations are no longer of a personal or family nature. In their dealings with one another, governments are entirely impersonal. What is equally important, the states participating in contemporary world affairs are not merely the Christian states of Europe, with their similar background of culture and history, which formerly made up the society of nations; now the world community also embraces Moslem, Hindu, Buddhist and other non-Christian peoples, whose ethical backgrounds vary widely. As heterogeneity has replaced homogeneity, the problem of creating and maintaining an ethical code among nations has been complicated immeasurably.

The crescendo of nationalism, especially since the French Revolution, has been another obstruction to the development of a sensitive ethical or legal system. Contemplating a given course of action, the ardent nationalist goes along with Stephen Decatur's oft-quoted statement, "Our country! In her intercourse with foreign nations may she always be in the right; but our country, right or wrong." He will lie, steal, and kill for the good of the nation, although his own personal ethical code will prevent him from committing such acts in order to promote his own good. He thus exalts his nation-state to a position superior to ethical codes. Whether he does so knowingly and blatantly like the German Nazis, or blindly like the more extreme nationalists of the democracies, the effect is much the same.

Sponsors of codes of conduct, whether ethical or legal, in world affairs must realize that what they are trying to do is to curb the use of the power which nations possess. They are trying to distinguish between the proper uses and the improper uses of power, permitting the one and prohibiting the other. Theoretically, they stand on solid ground, for such a distinction exists and can easily be defined in a broad way: power is justifiable, for instance, when employed for self-defense and it is objectionable when used for aggrandizement. Spelling out distinctions of this nature in the form of specific rules of law or ethics is a basic need of the society of nations. "Self-defense" and "aggression" are still hazy concepts, as the International Law Commission of the United Nations has revealed in its efforts, thus far futile, to define them.

Should the stupendous task of drafting ethical and legal codes ultimately prove successful, then the still more challenging problem must be faced of gaining respect for them. Will nations with power desist from its use in ways defined as unethical or illegal? Can a system of ethics or a rule of law be constructed which will keep a nation "good" when it can gain an important advantage by being "bad"?

The well-known journalist Mr. E. A. Mowrer, in *The Nightmare of American Foreign Policy*, has pointed out the similarity between the modern community of nations and the old-time frontier town or "roaring camp" of the American West. Like the wild western town, the world of today is weak in its political organization, unable to protect its members, to maintain order, or to secure justice. Self-protection being the only safeguard to life and limb, nations carry guns and use them to deter or to punish predatory neighbors. In these rigorous conditions of life every advantage must be seized by the nation that would live; law and ethics appear to nations as commendable goals for the future but wholly impracticable to those who want to stay alive today.

Here again is the problem of combining realism with idealism. Seeking to protect ourselves in the world as it is, we may also attempt to improve it for the future. The advocate of ethical and legal codes must realize that in the world as it is, nations will respect rules only so long as they are not called upon to make too serious a sacrifice; they will never obey any rule at the risk of life itself or of anything deemed necessary to life. To expect them to do so is not realistic. Facing these unpleasant facts of modern world politics will not, however, prevent one from trying to transform the community of nations from a roaring camp into a relatively safe and secure place.

What, then, is to be gained from the study and development of ethics and law in international relations? Surely no one would be so rash as to expect the quick emergence of a new world order of peace and justice. The provision of sound ethical and legal codes of conduct is only one of many changes necessary to the new order which, if they are fortunate, our children or grandchildren may experience. Equally important is it for people to learn to think without the prejudice and bias of nationalism, to discover that internationally as well as nationally ballots are superior to bullets as a form of power, to find out what an empty thing a nation's sovereignty can be, and to revise their thinking in many other ways. Codes of law and of ethics can eventually have a place only in a world fully capable of relying on them.

In the meantime, before codes of ethics and law can have the advantage of a mature world community capable of giving high respect to them, they will still have a limited utility. For one thing, they will supply norms of conduct which nations will not lightly ignore. Every nation, however evil its designs may be, even now prefers to be known as a respecter of established rules of conduct; a good reputation is as great an asset to a state as to an individual. For this reason no nation ever admits itself to be a violator; even Nazi Germany, fascist Italy, and militaristic Japan argued that they were circumspect, both ethically and legally, and tried to prove that their enemies alone were delinquent. Standards of conduct, whether of an ethical or legal character, which place upon nations the onus of justifying their actions are well worth having. However much President Wilson's notes to Germany on neutrality violations were scoffed at in World War I, there was something highly satisfying in being able to compel the Hohenzollern government to defend itself against well-founded charges that it had violated international law. The same satisfaction has attended charges by the United States against Red China of mistreating Americans. The alternative to rules of ethics and law that cannot be enforced but can be appealed to as bases for complaints and for reparation is no rules at all—an admission that any nation may do anything it pleases without protest or accusation by the aggrieved party or by the world community.

In some ways the present is an opportune time for attempting to improve the ethics and law of international conduct. For one thing, power in the sense of physical coercion has become so oversized with the new nuclear weapons that nations cannot afford to use it, and therefore are both in need of rational criteria of conduct and in a better frame of mind than ever before to accept them. This may be the reason why such terms as "moral force" and "moral strength" have worked their way into the terminology of world affairs. In his State of the Union address on January 9, 1952, President Truman asserted, "To meet the crisis which hangs over the world, we need many different kinds of strength—military, economic, political, and moral. And of all these, I am convinced that moral strength is the most vital."

Decent as we usually are in our outlook, even we in this country can benefit from a studied attention to ethics and law. For the first time in our history we are deep in power politics. On the intellectual side, men like George Kennan, Walter Lippmann, and Hans Morgenthau have been trying to educate us in the facts of power politics, and at last we have added the word "power" to our vocabulary. What is more, the United States now possesses vast power in the form of fighting forces and weapons, probably more than any other country. All this has not yet turned our heads and we do not appear at this juncture to have developed an undue admiration for physical might; in fact the American attitude toward the Anglo-French invasion of Egypt and toward the Russian massacres in Hungary late in 1956 showed an abhorrence of it. Nevertheless we need to be on the alert in maintaining acute ethical sensitivities, for it is easy for a nation with an excess of power to extol it, as almost every strong nation of the past at one time or another has done—Great Britain, France, Germany, and Japan. Swinging from one extreme to another is a tendency of Americans; from the abhorrence of might to its glorification would not be out of our character. Right now, with Soviet Russia as our potential enemy, we have a special temptation to drop our ethics and rely on armament, for communism respects no ethics or law. As Representative Joseph Martin of Massachusetts said 'way back in 1924, communism maintains itself "by untruth, suspicion, and heresy." However appropriate it may seem to "fight fire with fire," as the slogan goes, we need to remind ourselves that a nation does not eradicate unethical conduct on the part of others by resorting itself to unethical conduct. Ambassador Chester Bowles' generalization, in his *Diplomat's Report,* that "the most hardheaded and the most hopeful policy is one based on restraint, firmness, patience, and flexibility," is sound.

Conditions are now propitious for the development of rules of ethical and legal conduct for another reason, one which was not present even fifteen years ago—the many new, small states that have appeared in the world. Since World War II India, Pakistan, Burma, Ceylon, Indonesia, the Philippines, Syria, Lebanon, Jordan, Israel, the Sudan, Libya, Morocco, Tunisia, and the Gold Coast have emerged from declining empires; more, particularly in Africa, will soon become free. States which are weak and at the same time fearful of the great powers almost invariably have a predilection for rules of orderly conduct in which they can place some measure of trust. They can be counted upon to cooperate in this as in other movements in behalf of international justice.

The greatest opposition to a serious-minded effort to develop orderly rules of conduct would be encountered in the communist nations. But despite their willingness to violate rules if they believe they see a resulting advantage, it is pertinent to observe that Russia's leaders constantly talk in terms of ethics and law. Professor Dexter Perkins brought out this fact in *The American Approach to Foreign Policy,* saying that while Russia's rulers are "oblivious to any precept of international morality," they nevertheless "constantly talk in terms of such precepts, constantly invoke the Hitlerian device of describing other peoples as bellicose and sinister. . . ." All of this suggests that ideas of morality and law have become so firmly embedded in popular thinking that every government, however heinous its actions, feels the necessity for justifying itself both to its own people and to the world in terms of ethical and legal responsibility. If this be true, it is encouragement to those who would make it their business to develop rules of conduct.

How, if at all, can the churches relate themselves to the progressive development of rules of conduct in international relations? Certainly they have little to offer toward the construction of a better system of international law, except perhaps to express their support for the idea, as they have done from time to time. Report IV of the Amsterdam Assembly (1948), for instance, declared that "as within the nations, so in their relations with one another, the authority of the law must be recognized and established. International law clearly requires international institutions for its effectiveness." This kind of generalization clearly falls within the purview of church bodies, since it has no direct relationship to specific issues of policy.

The laborious job of working over the law as it stands and making suggestions for improvements belongs to experts of the type that no organization in this country could assemble except, perhaps, the American Bar Association and the American Society of International Law. The undertaking is in any case one in which governments must in one way or another take part through their appointed representatives, for it is they who are expected to obey the law. The United Nations wisely set up an International Law Commission several years ago to be responsible for the progressive development of the law. The fifteen experts who constitute the Commission have been at work on the subject, and they have issued a number of reports; because their progress has been slow, suggestions have been made to strengthen the Commission, but to little avail.

The churches' bailiwick is the ethical rather than the legal. These two aspects of conduct are, of course, related, even though less closely than in the days when the law of nature was generally accepted. The rules of international law, like those of national law, can be and usually are expressive of justice and therefore of ethical principles; when newly drafted codes of international law are anything more than a statement of the practice of nations, the drafters have in some degree used their concepts of justice, their ethical sense, to determine the new rules. Respect for an established law, too, is largely a matter of ethics. From these facts, it follows that whatever sharpens the ethical sensitivities of peoples contributes indirectly to a stronger system of law. The Amsterdam Assembly seemed to recognize this truth in its statement that the churches "have an important part in laying that common foundation of moral conviction without which any system of law will break down." Here again is an example of the dynamic potentialities in international affairs of the leaven of Christianity within the body politic.

The churches are well equipped to deal with the ethics of international conduct, even if not with international law. Here, indeed, is a field in which they might engage in much study and deliberation. Also it is an area in which they might undertake to make generalizations setting forth their findings. To go further, however, and to try to apply ethical codes or principles to specific disputes, such as the Anglo-French use of force in Egypt in 1956, would be to meddle dangerously with concrete issues.

Reference has been made in this chapter to the endorsement given by the Evanston Assembly of the World Council in 1954 to the need for an international ethos. The Report of Section IV also recognized the responsibility of Christian churches to do their part "to bring the guiding principles of international life into greater harmony with God's will." Then the Report went on to advance "tentatively" the following points as basic to an international ethos:

(1) All power carries responsibility and all nations are trustees of power which should be used for the common good.

(2) All nations are subject to moral law, and should strive to abide by the accepted principles of international law to develop this law and to enforce it through common action.

(3) All nations should honor their pledged word and international agreements into which they have entered.

(4) No nation in an international dispute has the right to be sole judge in its own cause or to resort to war to advance its policies, but should seek to settle disputes by direct negotiation or by submitting them to conciliation, arbitration or judicial settlement.

(5) All nations have a moral obligation to insure universal security and to this end should support measures designed to deny victory to a declared aggressor.

(6) All nations should recognize and safeguard the inherent dignity, worth and essential rights of the human person, without distinction as to race, sex, language or religion.

(7) Each nation should recognize the rights of every other nation, which observes such standards, to live by and proclaim its own political and social beliefs, provided that it does not seek by coercion, threat, infiltration or deception to impose these on other nations.

(8) All nations should recognize an obligation to share their scientific and technical skills with peoples in less developed regions, and to help the victims of disaster in other lands.

(9) All nations should strive to develop cordial relations with their neighbors, encourage friendly cultural and commercial dealings, and join in creative international efforts for human welfare.

This is probably the major effort of the Protestant churches to state a few basic ethical principles. Extremely general in character and somewhat platitudinous, these few statements could hardly be expected to make much of an impression on the world of nations. They do not take into account any conditioning or qualifying circumstances—the "ands," "ifs," and "buts" which always attend any ethical problem. For instance, the third rule listed, "All nations should honor their pledged word and international agreements into which they have entered," is no doubt correct as a generalization and is widely accepted. But what about an agreement which has been forced on a nation or entered into by a weak or backward government unaware of the implications of its act? Should the China of 1925 have honored indefinitely the old unequal treaties imposed upon its ignorant Manchu government by the imperialist states of the West? What about an agreement made by an earlier government within the state dominated by an alien ideology, perhaps fascism or communism? Should Italy today respect all the pledges made by Mussolini? If the communists were thrown out of Russia and succeeded by a genuine democracy, should the new government fulfill all the obligations earlier assumed by the communists? Should a government meet an obligation to do something wrong, as for instance Czechoslovakia's agreement in 1956 to supply Egypt with arms which would upset the power balance in the Middle East?

Ethical generalizations which do not allow for the special circumstances that invariably surround a concrete international problem can cause more trouble by the confusion they produce than could possibly be offset by the presence of a rule. Under the eighth rule above, calling upon nations to share their technical skills with peoples in less developed regions, the United States might be called upon to supply Soviet Russia, or her satellites, potential enemies in war, with technical information that could be used against us. Was this eventuality intended by the makers of the rule?

The makers of ethical codes must start with the adoption of criteria of some kind by which they can set up and measure the validity of their rules. What is there available for this purpose? The old law of nature was criticized on the ground that it was inexact, leaving too much to the subjective opinions of the men pronouncing it; what would be entirely right and harmonious to one person would seem wrong to another. Is there anything to take its place?

The impulse of Christian leaders is to attempt to apply the ethical principles enunciated by Christ to the acts of nations, either with or without the cooperation of the other great world religions. To what extent is it practicable to apply Christian ethics to national conduct? We must remind ourselves that Christian ethics are more than a collection of exhortations against the offenses of lying, stealing, and murder. They require the positive virtues of turning the other cheek when struck, giving your cloak to one who sues you at law and takes your coat, going two miles with him who compels you to go one, blessing him who curses you, and loving your enemy. They call for a type and degree of sacrifice completely ruinous to contemporary concepts of the "national interest." Do Christian leaders seriously advocate conduct that would enable our enemies to destroy us?

The incompatibility of Christian ethics with our present ideas of national interest, and with the tone and temper of contemporary world politics may be explained in either of two ways. In the first place, the ethics of Christ were recommended for individuals, not for nations. It was President Wilson's belief, however, that in ethical matters no distinction should be drawn between nations and individuals; this view has been expressed, too, by authorities of the Catholic Church and by others. This is a far cry from the opinions of Hegel, von Treitschke and that school of thought which extols the nation-state as superior to all codes of ethics. Whether the nation-states *ought* to heed the ethics laid down by Christ for the individual is an academic question; the fact is that they do not and could not without suffering annihilation. In practice, if not in theory, Christian ethics are often regarded by the nation-state as though they had no relevance to the world of diplomacy.

In the second place, the impossibility of bridging the gap between the ethical principles of Christ and the practice of nations suggests that the present structure of international society is fundamentally wrong. Although criticism of international society is by no means novel, this evidence of its weakness is one which has not been emphasized. The hypothesis that the more difficult compliance with Christian ethics is within a society, the less sound must be its structure, seems correct, that is if it be conceded that Christianity is applicable to the relationships of nations.

For other reasons it is clear that an acceptable system or code of international ethics cannot be based solely on Christian con-cepts. Christendom is not identical today with the community of nations, as it once was. No ethical principles could be universally applicable today unless they incorporated the ideas of Buddhist, Moslem, Hindu, and other religious groups. While we in this part of the world esteem Christian principles as adequate to the needs of right living, we must realize that they cannot be imposed on peoples who cherish their own system. This means first that, if the Christian churches are to strive for the maximum benefits of an ethical system in international relations, they must, after working on the subject nationally, consult with the religious leaders of the African and Asian nations within a world-wide agency of some kind. Second, the system of ethics produced must draw from the

ideas of many faiths, and cannot be expected to incorporate much
that is not common to all.

Cooperation among leaders of the world's great religions is by
no means a new idea. For instance, in 1948 a meeting in New
York City of representatives of Buddhism, Judaism, Christianity,
Islam, Taoism and Confucianism met together in the Conference
of Religion for Moral and Spiritual Support of the United Nations.
At this meeting Dr. Ralph W. Sockman, President of the Church
Peace Union, pointed to certain fundamentals underlying all religious faiths, such as a belief in one Creator, and a sense of right
and wrong which he called a "moral bedrock." Although the name
of the Conference appeared to imply that it would confine itself
to building up moral and spiritual support for the United Nations—
a proper sphere of action for religious groups—in fact it took up
subjects for whose treatment it was less well qualified and came
out with recommendations for changes in the structure of the
United Nations and for the limitation of armament.

Another approach to the problem of constructing an international ethical system would be to eliminate the religious basis of
ethics and employ utilitarian doctrines as a measure of conduct.
The query then would be, not whether Christ, Buddha, or some
other religious authority approved or disapproved a given course
of action, but rather what the effect of that action on the welfare
of mankind would be. Evidence of some application today of this
criterion to national conduct is seen in the tendency to condemn
war on the ground that it does not pay. Such statements as "Even
the victor is a loser in a modern war" and "Another war will be the
end of Western civilization" testify to utilitarianism at work in
popular thinking.

Another utilitarian principle might well be asserted, and occasionally is, to the effect that it pays a nation to deal fairly and
squarely with others. The nation which keeps its word, respects the
rights of others, and endeavors to conduct itself properly will gain
the confidences of others and the prospect of an international
atmosphere conducive to security and prosperity. Nazi Germany
proved both to herself and to the world that unconscionable behavior is unprofitable and will set in motion forces harmful to all.

The utilitarian criterion of conduct may seem at first glance to have a materialistic or secular basis and therefore not to deserve the attention of Christian leaders; further reflection will disclose, however, that this is not necessarily true. What more significant to the religionist could there be than evidence that the Creator so made the world that it pays men and nations to be decent in their relationships with others?

Professor John Dewey believed that utilitarianism is not likely to have much influence on the ethics of international conduct, because it is "too rationalistic" and because "it assumes in an exclusive way that men are governed by considerations of advantage, of profit and loss." He argued that, although utilitarian doctrines can be a basis for the determination of the ethical, there remains the problem of "linking up with the moral the motives that will make it prevail in conduct." The question of motivation in conduct, of getting adherence to established moral standards, is always a problem and always will be, whatever the method employed for setting up standards. If religious beliefs can be a factor in motivation, then the tie between utilitarian rules of conduct and respect for those rules will be stronger when utilitarianism is looked upon as having a religious foundation rather than a purely materialistic basis.

My purpose in this discussion is not to urge the adoption of any particular approach to the problem of constructing an international ethical system, but rather to point out the complexity of the subject and to examine available criteria for the determination of what is right and what is wrong in the conduct of nations. The churches, should they decide to give closer attention to standards of national conduct, must think their way through the problems which have been mentioned in this chapter.

XIII

The Ecumenical Movement

Of potential significance to the future of international relations is the ecumenical movement of our times. Prior to the Reformation, Christianity in the Western world was a unified movement, held together by the organization of the Catholic Church. The Reformation ended all this, splitting Christendom into fragments and leading in some cases to the establishment of national churches. The universal quality of the Christian faith was thus destroyed.

During recent decades Christianity has been regaining the sense of unity which it once had, as international or world conferences of church groups, and the enterprises which they have sponsored, have spread and flourished. Although there had been forerunners of this ecumenical movement in the form of Bible societies, missionary activities, the Evangelical Alliance, and other cooperative organizations, its present era is usually dated back to 1910, when the Missionary Conference of the Protestant Churches met at Edinburgh; the International Missionary Council grew out of this meeting. In the summer of 1914 a "peace conference" was planned and organized by the Church Peace Union, a body created in the United States and endowed by Mr. Andrew Carnegie.

After World War I interest in the integration of Christianity deepened, and more and more international conferences of Christians were held. Prominent among them were the Conference on Life and Work at Stockholm (1925) and the Conference on Faith and Order held at Lausanne (1927), both including the Eastern

Orthodox churches along with most of the Protestant denominations. The Roman Catholic Church did not take part. Again in 1937 a Conference on Faith and Order met, on this occasion at Oxford, England; and in the same year a second Conference on Life and Work took place, convening at Edinburgh. At this time the two movements—that on faith and order, and that on life and work—merged into one body, the World Council of Churches, to which frequent references have been made in earlier chapters.

Two important ecumenical meetings were held just before World War II. In December, 1938, the International Missionary Council organized a conference at Madras, India, which drew unusual attention because of the large representation of the churches of Africa and Asia. Then in July and August, 1939, a Youth Conference met at Amsterdam, the Netherlands, prepared and carried out mainly by the World Council of Churches; approximately 1,500 delegates, mainly young people under thirty years of age, attended this meeting.

The present ecumenical structure of Christendom was set up at the Amsterdam World Assembly in 1948. One hundred and thirty-five churches were represented there; sixteen others accepted the invitation to send delegates, but failed to do so. Approximately 1,500 people attended the sessions, of whom 352 were delegates, an equal number were alternates, and the remainder were consultants and visitors. These people came from forty-four countries, including nations recently defeated in war—Germany, Japan, and Italy; none came from the Soviet Union or its satellites in eastern Europe. All of the principal denominations of the Christian faith were represented except the Roman Catholic, the Orthodox Catholic, and the Southern Baptist; these three had "unofficial observers" in attendance. For discussion purposes this Assembly was organized into four sections, each of which worked out a "Report" that was submitted to the main body for discussion and acceptance.

Ecumenical organization was placed upon a permanent basis at Amsterdam. The World Council of Churches, which had hitherto been an improvised agency, was formally constituted to carry forward the joint enterprises of the churches. The World Assembly, the Commission of the Churches on International Affairs, and

several other organs to be mentioned later, were also given a constitutional basis in this new structure of Christendom.

Soon after the Amsterdam Assembly came to an end, the study
department of the World Council began preparing for a second
Assembly. In August, 1954, the second Assembly met and de-
liberated on the campus of Northwestern University for a period
of seventeen days; its sessions were attended by 1,242 men and
women, of whom 502 were official delegates. They spoke for 132
of the 163 Protestant and Orthodox communions of the World
Council of Churches; twenty-five "unofficial observers" from other
communions were also present. Discussions centered on the theme
"Christ—the Hope of the World." Again six sections worked on
subthemes, and their reports came out under the following titles:
"Faith and Order"; "Evangelism"; "Social Questions"; "International Affairs"; "Intergroup Relations"; and the "Laity." The
Assembly also issued a "Message to Christians" everywhere, affirming "our faith in Jesus Christ as the hope of the world." What was
said and done at this Evanston Assembly probably attracted the
attention of the world more than any other religious event in recent
history. *Time* reported that "in the twentieth century it was big
news that people saw a hope in Christianity."

Frequent allusions to the special interest of the World Council
of Churches in international problems have been made earlier.
Both the Amsterdam Assembly (1948) and the Evanston Assembly
(1954) discussed international affairs in Section IV, set up for that
purpose, and both issued reports pointing out the relation of
Christianity to contemporary issues. Reference has also been made
in other connections to the Committee of the Churches on International Affairs which has been operating under the World
Council; this C.C.I.A. had been created in 1946 by a Joint Committee of the World Council and the International Missionary
Council.

Although the World Council of Churches, together with its
subsidiary agencies, must be regarded as the main expression of the
ecumenical movement, others should not be overlooked. World
meetings of separate denominational groups—the Baptists, Metho-
dists, Congregationalists, Presbyterians, and others—have been

held from time to time. While they are usually less interested in social and international problems than is the World Council, they have expressed themselves occasionally on subjects of this nature. For instance, in 1950 the Eighth Congress of the Baptist World Alliance, then forty-five years old, spoke out against racial segregation in South Africa and in the United States, and advocated American ratification of the Genocide Convention. Critics of world-wide denominational conferences will agree with one of the editors of the *Christian Century* (August 16, 1950) that they represent "sectarianism raised to the international level." Nevertheless they carry much the same significance to international relations as does the World Council, bringing together the peoples of many lands for an exchange of views.

The importance of the ecumenical movement to foreign affairs is not related to the opinions expressed upon concrete issues of policy, whether by the Assembly of the World Council, the C.C.I.A., or denominational bodies; these I have discussed earlier in this book. To date, ecumenical bodies have made little, if any, contribution by means of formal educational efforts to the quality of the body politic within the nations whose churches participate; this the future may bring, especially from the World Council. Clearly an ecumenical effort to strengthen the bodies politic of the nations would have advantages over national efforts by the churches, ensuring as it would the presentation in discussions of a greater variety of points of view, and almost certainly diminishing the bias of nationalism.

In its present form, the ecumenical movement's finest contributions to a more stable world order are by-products of that intermingling of Christian peoples from all over the world which, indeed, is its life blood. "Spectacular" is not too strong an adjective to apply to the personnel of the Assemblies held at Amsterdam and Evanston; the third Assembly scheduled for 1960 will doubtless be equally dramatic. Here Americans strike up a friendly acquaintance with Syrians, Japanese, Belgians, Danes, and Swedes. A German and a Frenchman sit under a tree and talk about philosophy, religion, or perhaps the problem of the Saar Basin. In a committee or a subcommittee, religionists from many nations discuss communism, colonialism, or nationalism, sometimes agreeing and on other occasions clashing sharply. At home again in their respective countries, the delegates relay these experiences on to their fellows.

In addition to the Assembly sessions there are a great variety of other meetings under the aegis of the World Council. The Council itself holds annual sessions. From time to time the executive committee of the Council meets together, where again there are international contacts among people of good will. Officers of the Council travel about from country to country on business; for instance, a few years ago Rajah B. Manikam was selected by the World Council and the International Missionary Council as a joint secretary for eastern Asia to visit the churches of that area. Special conferences of one sort or another are frequently called together: early in 1955 the World Council's executive committee authorized the C.C.I.A. to call a meeting of representative churchmen from western Europe to discuss German rearmament. Another example of regional activities was the conference held a few years ago of Evangelical churches at Torre Pellice, Italy, attended by sixty delegates from France, Italy, Spain, Portugal, Belgium, and Switzerland. In the summer of 1956 a group of working committees of the World Council met in Herrenalb, Germany. The Council has thirty members of its staff now making surveys in Japan, Indonesia, India, Egypt, Lebanon, the Gold Coast, Northern Rhodesia, South Africa, and Brazil. These surveys are to be completed by 1960, when the third Assembly meets.

Contacts of this nature are also promoted by denominational gatherings. The world Christian youth movements, the Y.M.C.A. and the Y.W.C.A., in like manner send people across national boundaries to mingle with others of their age group in a common cause.

Significant, too, within the ecumenical movement is the student exchange system for seminaries that has been worked out by the World Council of Churches. In the school year 1950–1951 there were 121 seminary students exchanged by the United States and the nations of Europe; in addition there were many exchanges among the European countries themselves. Thirty-six Europeans were studying in American seminaries and two in Canada. Nineteen alien students were enrolled in British seminaries. In Germany there were fifteen American, British, French, Swedish, and Swiss students living on scholarships supplied by German churches.

Obviously the effect which this mingling of people with people produces upon the thinking of the participants cannot be measured in any precise way. The Government of the United States has attested its conviction that contacts between the peoples of different nations does influence outlook and points of view by its extensive program of educational and cultural exchange. Our officials maintain that an exchange of students, teachers, artists, musicians, and actors will lead to a better understanding abroad of our way of life and of our policies, as well as to a stronger appreciation by us of the cultures of others. In September, 1956, President Eisenhower told one hundred distinguished Americans representing forty fields of endeavor who were about to take part in these activities, "There is no more important work than that in which we are asking you to participate." Elaborating on the point, the President said that because "no people want war . . . the problem is for people to get together and leap governments—if necessary to evade governments—to work out not one method but thousands of methods by which people can gradually learn a little bit more of each other." Director Theodore Streibert of the United States Information Agency, too, has spoken favorably of the "people-to-people" idea as one productive of friendship among nations.

Whether or not the mingling of peoples is in fact a constructive force in international relations depends, of course, on who the individuals are that get together. An army of occupation in Germany or American troops located at bases in Iceland can produce misunderstanding rather than friendliness. American tourists in Europe have often conducted themselves so offensively as to arouse the indignation and ill will of native peoples. To state as axiomatic that international good will follows the interchange of students, teachers, musicians, executives, or even religious leaders is to err and mislead. The result depends on the character of the individuals concerned, whether they are tolerant or bigoted, outgoing or self-centered, kindly or inconsiderate, tactful or crude.

We may safely assume that those who take part in ecumenical activities are the type of men and women who will reflect credit upon their respective countries of origin. Herein lies the main reason for looking upon the movement as one potentially constructive in international relations. Its stimulus is a Christian faith so impelling that men and women will hurdle national boundaries and even national prejudices in order to be able to work with the people of other countries in a common cause. Attitudes better attuned for harmonious relationships with alien peoples would be difficult to prescribe.

The statement is often made that, in order to have an orderly world governed by law, there must first be a popular feeling that in fact the world is one community. Mr. W. P. Merrill asserted some years ago that "we must have a world system or world community, very real, even if intangible, before institutions and laws and agreements can be effective and lasting." How better than by the extensive ecumenical activities of today can the idea of a world community be stimulated? The integration of the Christian churches is a proper starting point for the integration of the nations into the unity which the miracles of science and the holocaust of modern warfare demand.

The ecumenical program embraces for all practical purposes the missionary effort. In Mr. Charles Leber's words, "The ecumenical movement and the missionary enterprise are essentially one and the same." For one thing the Christian churches of many countries which take part in the movement were themselves the product of missionary work. A present purpose of the movement is to strengthen and extend missionary activities. Section II of the Evanston Assembly took up the subject of the "Evangelizing Church," emphasizing the world-wide task of evangelism and the serious obstacles to it now encountered in Asia and Africa in the renascence of non-Christian faiths, the new native nationalism, and the spread of antagonistic political ideologies. Evidence that the missionary enterprise has not been discouraged is furnished by the fact that, as of 1952, there were 37,500 Protestant missionaries abroad, an impressive number but considerably smaller than the Catholic representation.

Although a detailed assessment of the effect of the missionary enterprise upon international relations could not be attempted, it is possible to point up a few pertinent facts. In the first place, through the missionary enterprise the churches have for many years carried on programs of native improvement which have won the good will of millions of people and in some cases the confidence of governments. In effect the churches have carried on a Point Four project of their own, bringing to Asians and Africans education, sanitation, medical assistance, skill in some of the crafts such as weaving, as well as Christianity—all lines of welfare toward which the imperialist governments of the West were for years much too indifferent in the colonial areas. In his *Imperialism and World Politics* (1927) Parker Thomas Moon said, "Something like a million Negroes are now receiving some sort of schooling in the African colonies, largely thanks to the devoted efforts of Catholic and Protestant missionaries, while in Asia and the East Indies many millions are being educated." Although these activities occasionally aroused suspicion among the natives or the local authorities, for the most part they were accepted with gratitude. The good will which they generated, however, was often more than offset by Western traders who carried in their cargoes liquor and weapons, and by soldiers and civil service men who brought tyranny and war.

Years ago many missionaries increased the complications of the international relations of their time, with resulting complications today, by sponsoring imperialism. To quote again from Parker Thomas Moon's book, "Going out to preach a kingdom not of this world, missionaries found themselves often builders of very earthly empires." The churches and their missionaries often saw in the extension of Western governmental methods to pagan areas advantages to their efforts in the way of protection and the maintenance of order. Livingstone ardently advocated the establishment of British rule in Africa so that slavery there might be abolished and Christianity carried to the natives. Of the German missionary Fabri in southwest Africa during Bismarck's time, it has been said that he "converted more Germans to the cause of imperialism than natives to the Christian faith."

We must hasten to add that, if the churches and their missionaries were once in error in their support of imperialism, this is not the case today. As demands for independence and self-government have been raised by native peoples, the churches have frequently voiced their sympathy with the cause.

Nowadays missionaries are sometimes accused of taking part in the movement to stem the progress of communism and anti-Western sentiment in Asia and Africa. Mr. Stanley Rowland, Jr., of the *New York Times,* in the issue of May 14, 1956, explained at some length the ways in which they endeavor to meet the communist accusation that they are apostles of colonialism and "white supremacy." He points out that the challenge is being met "by letting Asians and Africans do evangelical work, by building indigenous churches and native hierarchies, and by emphasis on relief, educational and medical work." These activities have been strengthened, as he explains, by the increasing cooperation of Protestant groups with one another. Missionaries are also trying "to dissociate Christianity from a white and Western orientation and associate it with struggles for equality and betterment by non-White peoples." Mr. Rowland believes that it is impossible to estimate the degree of success which such efforts have met. More indigenous Christian churches exist now than ever before; but the increase in the number of Christian followers within these areas has not kept pace with the rise in population figures. Missionaries have found themselves embarrassed in their efforts to foster the movement for self-determination and equality for all peoples by the fact of racial segregation in the South of the United States and in South Africa.

As Mr. P. O. Philip brought out in the August 15, 1956, issue of the *Christian Century,* missions in India have been under fire for their alleged identification with the cause of the West in international relations. A six-member committee appointed by the Indian Government reported in part as follows:

"Evangelization in India appears to be a part of the uniform world policy to revive Christendom for re-establishing Western supremacy and is not prompted by spiritual motives. The objective is apparently to create Christian minority pockets with a view to disrupting the solidarity of the non-Christian societies, and the mass conversion of a considerable section of *Adivasis* (aborigines) with the ulterior motive is fraught with danger to the security of the state."

The committee stated elsewhere in its report that "the manner in which the missionary movement goes on in certain places is clearly intended to serve some political purpose in the cold war." It concluded that "the best course for the Indian churches to follow is to establish a united independent Christian Church in India without being dependent on foreign support."

If these charges that missionaries are serving the political cause of the West are true, then we are witnessing in a new context how the church may harm itself by taking sides on contentious issues, even though it lends its support to what seems to be a "good" cause. If the charges are not well founded, they nevertheless constitute a fair warning to the church that in these days of tension it must keep itself clear of suspicion. To lose the opportunity to carry on its religious enterprise abroad by involvement in international problems would be a grave mistake.

Postscript

Thomas Bailey in *The Man in the Street* remarks, "If religion is important to us, and if foreign policy is also important to us, each is bound to have some influence on the other, for the two cannot be compartmented in our thinking." This truth is the basis of my contention that the churches' main area of operation in strengthening American policy must be the body politic. And of all the contributions which they can make to the body politic—and there are several, as I have pointed out—the finest is to provide it in the future, as in the past, with the leaven of Christianity. True, honest-to-goodness Christianity in the hearts and minds of the people will work its alchemy in foreign policy as surely as a base will neutralize an acid.

Nowadays, with a United Nations to support and with talk of a closer union of states, the concept of a world-wide body politic is gaining headway, one prepared morally, intellectually, and emotionally to keep the peace. The churches can play a part in nurturing this universal body of politics along to full growth. No better starting points could be suggested than the ecumenical movement and the promotion of an international ethical system.

To me, one of St. Paul's most eloquent exhortations is in his First Epistle to the Corinthians, a portion of which reads as follows:

"For the body is not one member, but many. If the foot shall say, Because I am not the hand, I am not of the body; is it therefore not of the body? And if the ear shall

143

say, Because I am not the eye, I am not of the body; is it therefore not of the body?"

St. Paul might have been talking of the body politic and used much the same logic, for it, too, is made up of many "members": the government; the church; the farmers; the factories; the railroads; the electorate; and the schools. Each has its own work to do, and the working of each is essential to all of the others. The church and the electorate by doing well their respective tasks will strengthen the government in all its activities, including foreign policy making, but neither can take over the function of the government. The work of the church is fundamental; in a very real way it is the heart, pumping life throughout the entire body politic. It has no cause to say, "Because I am not the government, therefore I am not of the body."

Index